THE NORWICH FREE ACADEMY V. NEW LONDON FOOTBALL RIVALRY

THE NORWICH FREE ACADEMY
— V. —
NEW LONDON FOOTBALL RIVALRY

BRIAN GIRASOLI

THE History PRESS

Published by The History Press
Charleston, SC 29403
www.historypress.net

Front cover photos courtesy of the *Norwich Bulletin*, the *New London Day*, Norwich Free Academy and NFA and Bulkeley/New London yearbooks.

First published 2012
e-book edition 2012

ISBN 978.1.61423.585.9
print ISBN 978.1.60949.542.8

Library of Congress CIP data applied for.

CONTENTS

INTRODUCTION

Route 32 is one of the few state routes that begin on the Connecticut coastline and reach to the Massachusetts border and beyond. Starting in New London, Route 32 follows the west bank of the Thames River into Norwich and continues northward into Willimantic, Mansfield, Ellington and Stafford. As far back as 1670, the road was used as a trail for the Mohegan and Pequot tribes, and by 1922, the road had become part of the New England Interstate system.

It also is the main road that intersects both the Whaling City (New London) and the Rose City (Norwich), two cities that are about thirteen miles apart. Over the years, Route 32 has allowed Norwich residents to work at Electric Boat, one of the coastline's largest employers. It has allowed New London residents to work at the Foxwoods and Mohegan Sun casinos.

Route 32 also has allowed the residents to see their high school football teams play each other. And Norwich and New London residents have been making the trek longer than fans of any other high school game in the country.

Beginning in 1875, Norwich Free Academy (NFA) and Bulkeley School—later New London High School—have met on the gridiron. This matchup is recognized as the oldest high school football game in the country. It has spanned generations that have pitted family against family. There have been instances where a father played for one side and the son played for the other.

Future National Football League (NFL) and college football players participated in this rivalry. So have high-ranking military officials. Teachers and future coaches got their starts in this game.

For the last decade, the game has taken its place as the final regular-season game on Thanksgiving Day. While the crowds are not as large as they were forty or fifty years ago, a few thousand still hop on Route 32 and make the trip north or south to see the green and gold New London Whalers take on the red and white Norwich Free Academy Wildcats.

Chances are, there will be many more games to come.

HISTORY OF NORWICH FREE ACADEMY

On June 30, 1854, Norwich residents William M. Williams and his wife, Harriet Peck Williams, sold five acres off Crescent Street for $1 to be used for the construction of Norwich Free Academy. Almost $100,000 was raised for a building and a reserve fund for teachers' salaries and other costs, and construction began in earnest.

On October 21, 1856, Norwich Free Academy held its dedication. Norwich architect Evan Burdick designed a three-story, eleven-room structure. Students from Norwich and surrounding towns were eligible to attend the school but first had to pass a mandatory examination.

As the size of the classes grew, so did the campus. In the mid-1880s, notable Norwich resident and academy graduate William Slater financed a building in memory of his father, John Fox Slater. This became the Slater Memorial Museum, and today it is one of only two museums in the country that reside on a high school campus.

In 1895, construction was completed on a manual training building. Fifteen years later, the original 1856 building was demolished to make way for a larger classroom building. In 1906, the Converse Art Gallery was built. The Norton Gymnasium (1930) and Commercial Building (1933) also followed in the first half of the century. All of these buildings remain today, and along with newer buildings on campus, the two-thousand-plus students who attend from nine core towns and other outlying areas have plenty of room for their studies.

HISTORY OF BULKELEY

In 1849, Mr. Leonard H. Bulkeley willed $25,000 to a group of trustees, who were to allow the income to accumulate to $50,000. Once that was completed, a plot of land was to be bought and a building to be erected to provide free education to all male youths in New London. In 1871, that became a reality with the construction of Bulkeley High School, named after the benefactor.

Bulkeley's will also stated that the remaining funds were to be used to instruct the students "in morals and such branches of learning and science as prescribed by the trustees," according to the 1951 Bulkeley yearbook.

The original granite structure of the school was enlarged in the late 1890s and again thirty years later. In 1920, the trustees spent $90,000 on a second building that housed an auditorium and additional classrooms, and in 1934, a gymnasium was built, along with twelve classrooms.

At first, only students who lived in New London could attend Bulkeley, but out-of-towners were later permitted admission with a tuition payment.

In 1950, the board of trustees voted to sell the Bulkeley School to the City of New London for $200,000. Students from Bulkeley combined with the students of the vocational school, Chapman Tech, to form New London High School in time for the beginning of the 1951 school year.

In 1970, New London High School moved to its present location on Jefferson Avenue.

1
THE RIVALRY BEGINS
1875–1899

The first known football game between two collegiate teams occurred in 1874, when Harvard University met McGill University of Montreal. While many feel that an 1869 game between Rutgers and the College of New Jersey (later Princeton University) was the initial contest, that game more resembled rugby than what we know today as football; the final score was six "runs" to four.

During this time, rules that were closer to those of rugby took hold in the game. For example, the act of tapping the football off the foot of the center constituted the snap. It was not until Walter Camp's rule change in 1880 that the snap was moved from the center to the quarterback; this rule, in effect, remains today. Camp, who later became known as the "Father of American Football," also shrunk the roster from fifteen to eleven and established the line of scrimmage.

On June 5, 1875, Harvard played Tufts using rules that are closer to the game we know today in what is believed to have been the first American intercollegiate football game.

Three weeks prior, a high school team from Norwich Free Academy prepared to play a team from Bulkeley High School in New London. According to the morning newspaper, the *Norwich Courier*, on Wednesday, May 12, "The Bulkeley school boys will have a match game of football on Wednesday Afternoon."

No record of score was held for this game. In fact, for the first eight years of the rivalry, no results could be found of the games between the schools.

It was not until 1883 that regular reports began to surface. In the November 1, 1883 edition of the *New London Telegram*, the New London Northern Railroad offered tickets for fifty cents in advance of the game the following day. Listed under "City News" on page six of the November 2 *Norwich Morning Bulletin* was the following report: "The Free Academy foot ball team will play the Bulkeley High school team on Williams park at 3 p.m., Saturday."

Williams Park—which today is known as Chelsea Parade—is a large green located across the street from Norwich Free Academy, between Washington Street (Route 32) and Broadway. Because most newspapers did not print Sunday editions, the result of the game was not printed until the Monday, November 5 edition.

The *Bulletin* reported:

> *The Academy foot ball team played the Bulkeley High school team on Williams park in this city on Saturday afternoon. The game was witnessed by a crowd of spectators and was very exciting. The Academy team were* [sic] *winners by a score of 31 to 2. At the conclusion of the game a collation was served to the two teams by the female students of the Free Academy. The evening was agreeably spent, speeches and dancing following the refreshments. A return game will be played in New London next Saturday.*

Return, or revenge, games were common during this era as a way for the losing team to make up for a loss. Indeed, two weeks later, on November 17, the *Bulletin* announced that the Norwich Free Academy would play Bulkeley in New London.

In the Monday, November 19, edition, the *Bulletin* reported:

> *The Norwich Free Academy foot ball team went to New London Saturday to play a return game with the Bulkeley high school team whom they defeated in this city two weeks ago by a score of 31 to 2.*

> *Victory again favored the Academy team, they defeating the Bulkeley boys by a score of 33 to 2. Davies, Potter and Bidwell did the best work for the Academy team, Davies securing three touch-downs and Bidwell and Potter making good runs. Weaver did some splendid kicking for the New London team. After the game the young ladies of New London gave the boys a supper in the school building. Dancing followed, after which the Academy team were escorted to the train by the Bulkeleys and arrived at this city at 9 o'clock. They speak in no measured terms of the kind hospitality of the New London team.*

Bulkeley was a four-year school until 1885, when it became a three-year school until 1910. Because of its smaller student body, Bulkeley was not able to field a football team during these early years. In some years, the rivalry was carried on by teams from New London called the Bulkeley Alumni or New London YMCA.

It was these relaxed rules that defined the early game. In 1886, NFA officials discovered that a member of Bulkeley's faculty played in the game. It didn't matter; Norwich won the game, 13–6.

After a two-game NFA sweep in 1887 (26–0 and 38–4), Norwich and Bulkeley again played two games the next year. According to the Monday, October 29, 1888 edition of the *Bulletin*:

> *The foot ball game between the Free Academy and Bulkeley high school teams Saturday on Williams park, resulted in the victory of the home team by a score of sixteen to six. On account of darkness the game was closed twenty five minutes before the expiration of the full time. The Academy team will go to Worcester next Saturday.*

Three weeks later, on November 19, the teams met again at 2:00 p.m. in New London. "Never has there been so little difference in weight between the two teams as at present," wrote the *New London Day*. "The average weight of the Norwich team is about 147 pounds, that of Bulkeley being 140 pounds." For the first time, the *Bulletin*'s account included some opinion, something that would increase with regularity as the years went on:

The Norwich Free Academy foot ball team came to New London Saturday, though they had been notified that the Bulkeley school team would be unable to meet them to play a game. Tutor Drake organized a picked eleven and took the field against the visitors, but the visitors were too many for the New London novices and kicked the leather all over the ground. The game provided lots of fun for the spectators, but could hardly be called a game in accordance with recognized rules.

On November 4, 1889, the game was played at Cannonball Park in New London, which is on the banks of the Thames River. The contest ended early—not because of a lack of players or darkness but rather because the ball was lost in the middle of the game. Frederic H. Cranston, NFA class of 1891, told the following story to Paul Bradlaw, who was a member of the Norwich faculty from 1918 to 1965:

The game was supposedly played prior to 1890 at New London on a field off Pequot Avenue, near the harbor in the vicinity of the Admiral Billard Academy campus.

It was a cold, overcast November day. The game was in progress for some time when suddenly a snow squall of considerable intensity made its appearance. An Academy player punted the ball high in the air where it intermingled with the swirling snow flakes and sailed out of sight, nobody knew where.

Since nobody had another ball, the game stopped right there.

The game was listed as a 38–0 victory for Norwich. In fact, the final result is a common theme among the early years of the rivalry—Norwich is believed to have won every game but one up until 1910. It is reported that Bulkeley did win the October 28, 1891, game, 18–4, but that game may have included non-Bulkeley students. As written in the October 28, 1891 *Bulletin*:

New London 18, Norwich Free Academy 4

The academy sustained its second defeat at the hands of the New London team yesterday. The game is an example of what advantage

The 1891 NFA team beat Bulkeley, but Bulkeley—with the aid of some alumni—beat NFA, 18–4, in the return game. It was the last win for Bulkeley until 1910. *Courtesy of Norwich Free Academy.*

weight is to a foot ball team. The men on the New London line must have averaged from ten to twenty pounds heavier than the men against them. The teams were composed of

New London.		*Norwich Free Academy.*
Tracy,		*Dixon,*
Miner,		*Carey,*
Whittelsey,		*Terry,*
Freeman,	*Rushers,*	*Mr. Howes,*
Booth,		*Mr. Harding,*
Kaneen,		*Welch,*
Chappell,		*Mr. Fowler,*
		Murry,
Congdon,	*Quarter-back,*	*Lathrop,*
Hamill,		*Sevin,*
Congdon,	*Half-backs,*	*Rockwell,*
Graves,	*Full-back,*	*Arnold.*

The New London eleven made two touchdowns in the first half, one by Congdon and one by Hamill. Tracy kicked one goal. During the second half two more touchdowns were made by New London. Rockwell made a touch-down for the academy during the second half. The try at goal failed.

The academy team showed marked improvement since the game last Saturday.

Game at a Glance: October 30, 1897

The 1892 game was canceled because of "hoodlums," and for the next five seasons, no final score was given on record. That all changed on October 30, 1897, when Norwich won, 84–0. Under the headline "Free Academy 84, Bulkeley 0/Wretched Exhibition of Football/Very Loose Playing by Both Elevens/Academy Wins with Ease," the *Bulletin* reporter made no secret about what he thought of the game (and, yes, the question mark in the first sentence was the reporter's doing):

> *The most miserable exhibition of football ever seen on the academy gridiron was that of Saturday afternoon, when the Free academy eleven defeated a team (?) from the Bulkeley High school of New London by a score of 84 to 0. Neither side played football, but the academy can be credited with playing a shade better than their opponents. The whole contest was more of a farce than an athletic contest, and the number of touchdowns made was only limited by the time allowed.*
>
> *The game was called at 3.10, academy winning the toss and taking the north goal. Bulkeley kicked off, and after one or two downs Donohue made his way through the entire Bulkeley line and touched the ball back of the goal posts. Howe kicked the goal. Score, Academy, 6; Bulkeley, 0.*
>
> *The ball was again put in play and Academy held Bulkeley on the line, taking the ball on downs. Good runs by Buck and Keene brought the ball near Bulkeley's goal line, and Skelly took it over. Howe missed a try at goal. Academy, 10; Bulkeley, 0. Bulkeley kicked off again and buck made an end run of about 30 yards. Bulkeley won the ball on downs, but academy soon regained it on a fumble. Another 30-yards run by Buck took the ball over the line for another touchdown. Howe kicked a goal and the score stood: Academy, 16; Bulkeley, 0.*
>
> *The next skirmish had hardly opened when Donohue got the ball and aided by interference ran more than half the length of the field, touching it down behind the line. On account of a foul pass the ball was brought back and given to Bulkeley. Costello made a small gain, but Academy soon after got the ball on a fumble. Buck ran around the end and made*

the fourth touchdown. No fair catch was made on the punt out, and the score stood, Academy, 20; Bulkeley, 0.

The spectators by this time had lost all interest in the exhibition, which bore little resemblance to a football game. Buck and Skelly walked through the Bulkeley line for big gains, and the latter again took the ball over the line. Howe missed the goal. Score, Academy, 24, Bulkeley, 0.

Another run nearly half the length of the field by Donohue resulted in touchdown number 6. No goal was kicked and the score was Academy, 28; Bulkeley, 0. Donohue repeated his long distance running and another touchdown was scored for the academy, which, with a goal by Howe, made the score 34 to 0.

Skelly made the next touchdown, but no goal was kicked. Donohue took the pigskin over again and Howe kicked a goal. The half soon after ended, with the score 44 to 0 in Academy's favor.

The Second Half

The second half was practically a repetition of the first, touchdowns and goals being made in such rapid succession that the players could not keep track of the score.

Academy played in a little better form this half, while Bulkeley had naturally lost all heard in the contest. Skelly made one touchdown, Buck made three, Donohue one, Norman one and Howe one. The final score was Academy, 84; Bulkeley, 0.

For Academy, the best work was done by Skelly, Donohue, Buck and Keen, and for Bulkeley by Rathbone and Allen.

The line-up was as follows:

N.F.A.	*Positions.*	*Bulkeley*
Norman	*R.E.*	*Starr (Capt.)*
Bray, Gilbert	*R.T.*	*O'Neil*
Cornet	*R.G.*	*Rathbone, Randall*
Coit	*C*	*Comstock*
Perkins	*L.G.*	*Lewis*
Noyes (Capt.)	*L.T.*	*Duffy*
Buck	*L.E.*	*McGuire*
Keene	*Q.B.*	*Cronin*

The 1898 NFA team. One year after beating Bulkeley 84–0, this squad scored one touchdown and won 6–0. *Courtesy of Norwich Free Academy.*

Donohue	*R.H.*	*Reagan*
Skelly	*L.F.*	*Allen*
Howe	*F.B.*	*Costello*

Twenty-five and twenty minute halves. Umpire, W.K. Roe, Jr., new London; referee, C.D. Sevin, Norwich; linesman, Timothy Welch, Norwich; touchdowns, Donohue (5), Buck (5), Skelly (4), Norman, Howe. Goals from touchdowns, Howe (10).

NFA closed out the nineteenth century with a 6–0 win in 1898 and a 22–0 win in 1899.

2

BULKELEY MAKES IT A GAME

1900–1920

By 1900, high school football had begun to adopt rules that became more familiar. The playing field, called a "gridiron" because of its markings, was reduced to its present size of 120 yards by 53½ yards. Playing conditions, though, were far from ideal. According to an account in the 100th game program, "The 10-yard stripes often were inaccurate. An error of 112 inches, more or less, was quite common because of clothesline rope often used as a measuring line. The rope would stretch or shrink according to its moisture content."

Touchdowns, which had been marked originally as four points, increased to five and later six points. Kicks after touchdowns, first awarded as two points, later were reduced to one. The two-point safety, when a defensive player tackles an offensive player in the end zone, also was introduced.

All of these point totals exhibit the sheer scoring at will that Norwich Free Academy laid on Bulkeley in 1902. For the first two years of the twentieth century, the games were relatively tame. NFA won both, 5–0 in 1900 and 6–5 in 1901.

During the middle of the 1902 season, it appeared the Bulkeley game would not even happen. A *Bulletin* article from October 20 noted that the season might not even be completed on time because a number of players weren't attending school:

The 1902 NFA team. NFA put 130 points on Bulkeley in the first half before the Bulkeley coach waved the white towel early in the second half. It remains the most points ever scored in one game by one team in Connecticut history.

> *The report has been circulated about that the Academy football team will not be allowed to continue its schedule for the remainder of the season because of the actions of the members. After the game at Westerly, where they were defeated, only three of the team attended school the next morning. Oversleep and sprains were given as reasons. Because of this, it is believed, the team will be forced to end its season now.*

That appeared not to have happened because a few weeks after this article, NFA played Bulkeley. Although a newspaper account could not be found, what is known is that Norwich scored the first 130 points of the game—all in the first half! By the start of the second half, the Bulkeley coach had thrown in the towel, and the game ended as such.

While subsequent scores never reached this total, Norwich did continue to pile on the points, shutting out Bulkeley in the next four contests in 1904 and 1905.

Despite this one-sided affair over the first thirty-five years, Norwich was not immune to tricks of its own. In 1909, NFA trailed by a touchdown late in the game. The scorekeeper, a Norwich rooter, took it upon himself to help his team. He "accidentally" allowed the clock to run over, which

The 1909 NFA team that beat Bulkeley, 17–6. *Courtesy of Norwich Free Academy.*

helped Norwich score the tying touchdown, making it 12–12. It was then that the scorekeeper announced the time had expired.

Finally, in 1910, Bulkeley snapped its losing streak. Even though Bulkeley High School had switched to a four-year curriculum by this time, the help of several college boys home on vacation sealed the win. Captain S. Victor Prince, who later became the judge of probate for the New London district, scored the lone touchdown in a 6–0 win for Bulkeley.

Game at a Glance: November 4, 1911

From subjective timekeepers to adults who suited up, the games of this series up to this point did not elicit much of a cry from either side.

That all changed in 1911. The uproar caused in this first meeting of 1911 reflected the importance football was gaining all over this country at every level.

The play in question was a disputed touchdown that originally was nullified, allowing Bulkeley to win, 11–5. An Academy player recovered a muffed punt in the Bulkeley end zone for a five-point touchdown, and an extra point would have tied the game.

The referee ruled that the kick didn't go twenty yards, thus nullifying the touchdown. Norwich protested the ruling, appealing to the highest football expert at the time, Walter Camp. In responding to Norwich officials, Camp decided the dispute in favor of NFA, and thus the tie stood.

In the Monday, November 6 edition, under the headline "Game went to Bulkeley, 11–5," the *Norwich Morning Bulletin* reported the following:

> *Handicapped by Injuries, Academy Put Up a Brave Fight—Referee's Decision Cuts Off One Touchdown—Academy Plays Under Protest—Smith Breaks Collar Bone, Donnelly a Toe—Flaherty and Swan Individual Stars.*
>
> *Bulkeley made good on its chance against the Academy Saturday afternoon on Cannonball park, New London, defeating the Norwich Free Academy football team 11 to 5, in a game that was so close that a little shift in luck one way or the other might have returned either team the winner. With substitutes at both ends of the Academy line who had to go in with only one day's previous practice, the Academy machine was very much out of gear and the Bulkeley eleven should have swamped the Academy team by a much more conclusive showing to make it appear that they would have won with the academy at full strength or that they can win when the teams come together again.*
>
> *For all that, it was the best team and played the best football that Bulkeley has shown in years. It had a puzzling shift formation that was a ground gainer, and it was alert in spotting the Academy plays, blocking half a dozen different forward passes toward the end of the game through the alertness of Keefe and Crowley.*
>
> *With the score against them in the last half, the Academy kept up its fighting spirit and opened up an attack that at one time promised to bring them victory, and they were a fighting combination to the last.*
>
> *The game was played out under a protest by acting Captain McCormick that the Academy should be allowed another touchdown.*

Referee Hahn ruled that a punt on which the touchdown was made should have gone 20 yards, but nothing was found in the rules by a search made during the game to back him up in his decision. The play was on a low, short punt made over the line, which a Bulkeley man fumbled, pushing the ball up against an Academy runner, from whom it bounded back across the Bulkeley goal line, recovered by an Academy player and claimed as a touchdown. After a short argument on the point the referee refused to allow the score and passed over the rule book to Mr. McCoy of Bulkeley, who spent the afternoon trying to locate the rule, but had not found it by the time the game ended.

In the scoring the Academy did the first work, putting over a touchdown after eight minutes of play in the first period. McCormick made the first touchdown but missed the kick for goal. Flaherty put Bulkeley in the lead, 6 to 5, by making a touchdown, and kicking the goal close to the end of the season period. In the middle of the last period Flaherty on a forward pass made the final touchdown for Bulkeley, but missed the kick for goal from straight in front of the crossbar.

The game was as full of features as a county fair is of prize pumpkins. In the emergency that the Academy was in through the injury to Captain Gebrath, Russell Smith volunteered to go in at right end. Smith broke his collarbone in the first day of practice this season and has not been in the lineup since then. He had the same unfortunate experience again on Saturday, being forced to retire when the bone was broken again, but he was in the game long enough to be the hero of a sensational catch of a forward pass and a run of 20 yards after making the catch which brought the ball to Bulkeley's 25 yard line and gave the Academy its chance to score.

A long, lanky youth by the name of Bixler, wearing a yellow chrysanthemum the size of a wash basin, led the Bulkeley cheering section with a cornet, bass and snare drum to help out. Franklin Lord was the cheer leader for the Academy and the crowd of several hundred students kept things warmed up at all times in the cheering line.

Bulkeley suffered from injuries also in having Donnelly, their fastest halfback, break a toe, so that he alternated throughout the game with Casey, each going in for a few minutes at a time.

Flaherty loomed up as about half the Bulkeley team. He did all the punting, caught all the Academy kicks and was all over the field making tackles. It was a great day also for Sammy Lawrence at guard, as he was frequently down the field ahead of the Bulkeley ends and downing Academy catchers of punts. With the two green ends in the Academy lineup it was easy for the Bulkeley line to work their skin tackle plays on which Flaherty invariably came through till he was stopped by the secondary offense, and at the same time the Bulkeley players sifted around when the Academy had the ball and usually got McCormick before he had a chance to hit the line. They kept the Academy star chained down so that his gains were little during the game.

Quarterback Swan was the only ground gainer for the Academy on the running game, reeling off runs of 15 to 20 yards, besides playing a star game on the defense in tackling the Bulkeley men who were under way for dashes around the end.

Only Elliott and Herbert of the Academy line seemed able to get out to do any work in the open and it was Elliott who got Donnelly when this fast New London runner had dodged through nearly the whole Academy team for a 50-yard run that looked like a sure touchdown. That run was the turning point in the struggle, as up to that time the Academy had been outplaying Bulkeley and keeping the ball in Bulkeley territory. Bulkeley's other chance came in the last period when Porter misjudged one of Flaherty's punts. The ball struck the ground in front of Porter, flying away into a Bulkeley man's hand near the center of the field. On the next play or two a forward pass to Flaherty directly over center gave the New London player a clear field to the goal line and touchdown.

The plays that scored the touchdowns were the following:

FIRST PERIOD

In the absence of Captain Gebrath from the Academy lineup, McCormick was acting captain. Captain Costello of Bulkeley won the toss and chose to receive. McCormick kicked off and Bulkeley lost the ball on a fumble on the first scrimmage. Academy started to advance up the field, which put them in position to try a place kick for goal, but Bulkeley got through and blocked the kick. After an exchange of punts, McCormick from the center of the field shot a beautiful forward pass to Smith, who ran with it 20 yards before he was downed on Bulkeley's 20-yard line. Swan made 10 through center, and Herbert took the ball around through tackle, dropped it when he was tackled, but Smith saved it for the Academy on Bulkeley's 5-yard line. One try failed, but on the next McCormick went over for the touchdown. He missed the goal.

Second Period
Bulkeley started the second period with the ball in hand on its own 12-yard line. After several punts, a 50-yard dash by Donnelly carried the ball to the Academy's 20 yard line, from which Flaherty carried it over in four rushes for short gains each time. He kicked the goal, putting Bulkeley in the lead, 6 to 5. Smith's collarbone was broken at this point in the game. His place at end was taken by Porter and Kinney went in at guard. There was no further scoring in this period.

Third Period
In the third period came the play on which the Academy claimed the touchdown that was not allowed by the referee. A 40-yard run by Swan outside of Bulkeley's left end, flinging off tackler after tackler, was the individual feature of the period.

Fourth Period
The fourth period started on Bulkeley's 25 yard line, Bulkeley's ball. Soon after the ball opened Flaherty punted, Porter misjudging the sailing ball and a Bulkeley man recovered it for a substantial game. A good gain by a forward pass to Costello, a short gain by Keefe and a forward pass to Flaherty on which he scooted to the touchdown without being tackled, made Bulkeley's final touchdown. Flaherty missed kicking the goal. Academy tried desperately to even it up in the remaining time, but without result. The lineups and summary:

Academy	*Bulkeley*
Smith, Porter RE	*Reeves, LE*
Herbert RT	*Selikowitch, LT*
Potter, Kisney RG	*Lawrence LG*
Jackson C	*Huntley C*
Bliss LG	*McCarthy RG*
Elliott LF	*Schwartz RT*
Boyd	*Capt. Costello RE*
Swan QB	*Keefe QB*
Coughlin LHB	*Crowley LHB*
McCormick RHB	*Casey, Donnelly RHB*
Ricketts FB	*Flaherty FB*

Summary: Score, Bulkeley, 11, Academy, 5; touchdowns, Flaherty, 2, for Bulkeley, McCormick, 1, for Academy; goals kicked from touchdown, Flaherty, 1; goals missed from touchdown, Flaherty, 1, McCormick, 1, referee, C.A. Hahn of Brown; time, 10 and 12 minute periods.

The second game, played on Saturday, November 25, ended in a scoreless tie. According to the *Bulletin*, NFA fumbled twice at Bulkeley's one-yard line, and Norwich also missed four field goal attempts.

Bulkeley began its first winning streak in 1912, beating Norwich, 23–0 and 14–13. After a scoreless tie on November 10, 1913, Bulkeley won two weeks later, 14–0. The winning streak bumped up to six games with 26–0 and 20–0 victories in 1914.

Norwich put an end to its losing streak in 1915, winning by scores of 9–0 and 14–7. The first game featured a twenty-five-yard drop-kick field goal from Joe Hull, along with some heady play that prompted the *Bulletin* reporter to note the following:

> *Through the clear-sightedness of Joe Hull, who noticed that the opposing line was becoming more sieve-like, he hurried the backfield men against the line until the uprights came within view. Within four yards of the chalk line, J. Bradford Ricketts squeezed through a barn door prepared by "Stonewall" Jackson and "Achilles" Mullen for the first touchdown the Academy has scored since 1913.*

Season at a Glance: 1916

Five years after a referee's call changed the outcome, controversy again erupted in the first meeting of the 1916 season, on November 4. The Norwich placekicker, Lawrence J. "Chick" Stanley, went to try for a point-after-touchdown that would have given his team the lead. He went to move the ball to try for a better position, but the referee blew his whistle, believing that movement of the ball constituted an attempt to kick the ball. The play was whistled dead, negating an opportunity for Norwich to take the lead, and the game ended in a 6–6 tie.

The Monday, November 6 edition of the *Bulletin*, under the headline "Academy Held to a Tie," reported:

> *Bulkeley High Sprung a Surprise—Score 6 to 6—NFA's Play Failed to Come Up to Season's Standard—Both Teams Fumbled Considerable*
>
> *Bulkeley High threw a scare into the Academy in every sense of the word Saturday on the campus and held the red and white boys to a tie, outplaying them in the early stages of the game which unnerved NFA, but the old red and white fighting spirit was revived in the latter part of the game which staved off defeat. Referee Crowley erred when Stanley tried to kick a goal after a touchdown had been scored which might have meant victory. Stanley was sent to kick and he walked up to the ball to place it in a better position and in so doing the referee blew the whistle for the kick, naturally the crowd went wild.*
>
> *The New Londoners outweighed the Academy and were strong on the defense, breaking up many a good play. Right from the start, the visiting aggregation ran into a bunch of luck on recovering flunk fumbles which resulted in a score. Stanley and Bendett pulled off several long runs which revived the fighting spirit but someone would muss up things with a fumble. Stanley punting for the Academy was unable to get a good chance to boot the oval as the opposing linesman sifted through quite frequently thus hurrying the kick.*
>
> *At the beginning of the second quarter apparently the Academy had struck their stride, they started off with a rush recovering a fumble. All three backs tore off substantial gains only to have the jig thrown up by a poor pass*

or fumble. Again at the opening of the third quarter it looked as if the boys had met their own and were bound to show the color. They rallied strong, Keefe rushed the kickoff back twenty yards. Stanley on the first play tore off five yards around the end but the ball was lost on a fumble. Both Stanley and Bendett reeled off big gains and before the quarter ended the ball was placed within the shadows of the Bulkeley goal pasts just two yards within the chalk line and at the opening of the quarter Stanley and Bendett on successive rushes pushed the ball over, Bendett carrying the ball over.

In the final Bulkeley had a session at fumbles and just as time was called Oat caught a forward pass which netted 35 yards. Oat put up a good game throughout and has the markings of a good end.

Between the halves the Academy students swarmed the field, cheered and sang songs. The lineup:

NFA		*Bulkeley*
Parker	*Left End*	*Bradshaw*
Wilcox	*Left Tackle*	*Gallup*
Kozlowski	*Left Guard*	*Tovlin*
Eastwood	*Center*	*May, Capt.*
Senft	*Right Guard*	*Britton*
McMillan, Cap	*Right Tackle*	*Lawski*
Oat	*Right End*	*Sullivan*
Keefe	*Quarter Back*	*Mellon*
Stanley	*Right Half Back*	*Donnelly*
Graham	*Full Back*	*Redden*
Bendett	*Left Half Back*	*Whitcomb*

Referee—Crowley from Westerly.
Umpire—Ebbs from Rhode Island State. Time Keeper Alofsin
Field linesman—W. Stanley
Linesmen: Hert and Harrington.
Substitutes for Bulkeley—Glenn (left halfback) for Whitcomb; Oneal (left tackle) for Gallup; Davis (right guard) for Britton.
Substitutes for NFA—Ferguson for Oat.

Two weeks later, Stanley, a senior, atoned for the error by breaking the school record with a fifty-yard field goal. The previous school record, by

J. Aiken in 1890, was 132 feet, 4 inches (distances were not measured in yards yet). According to longtime Norwich teacher Paul Bradlaw, the kick was used as a teaching moment:

> *Stanley's feat gained national recognition in scholastic sports. What made the field goal unique was the angle from which it was kicked.*
>
> *Toward the end of the game, which was played at Plant Field in New London, Chick slammed the ball through the uprights from the 42-yard line with the ball spotted on the right sideline.*
>
> *Worked out in Pop Congdon's math class after the classic game, the kick was found to have traveled 149 feet. The angle from the sideline was approximately 31 degrees and the target distance between the uprights was narrowed to 15.7 feet.*

Under the headline "Academy Defeats Bulkeley," the November 20 edition of the *Bulletin* reported the following:

> *NFA Boys Score 10 Points in Last Quarter—Stanley and Ricketts Ripped New London's Defense—Chick Scored Difficult Field Goal.*
>
> *After withstanding the battering and hammering of the Academy backfield for three quarters, Bulkeley's defense collapsed with a cave in that that was ultimate, resulting in the Academy scoring a touchdown and field at Plant field, New London Saturday. It was in the final quarter that the Academy struck the crushing blows. Stanley, Graham and Ricketts, the heroes of the contest tore off repeated gains until Stanley rushed across the coveted chalk line. From then on the Bulkeley eleven lost heart and to rub it in a bit Stanley drop kicked a goal from a very difficult angle.*
>
> *The first three quarters the ball traveled up and down the field, neither team having outclassed the other. But at the opening of the last quarter things began to look different. The red and white came on the field with renewed fighting spirits and this spirit reigned supreme until the final whistle was blown.*
>
> *After the game the Academy students gave a demonstration in New London, parading the city over 100 strong, including a large number of the fair sex.*

After parading the main streets of the city here they adjourned to the campus where a large bonfire with speeches attracted a large crowd.

First Quarter

NFA received the kick-off. Stanley ran it back to his own 25-yard line, with good interference.

The Bulkeley line held and Stanley was forced to punt. Mallon fumbled the ball, but recovered it before Sears could get it. Donnelly made the only gain for Bulkeley, plunging through guard for five yards. Keefe got Bulkeley's punt and ran it back five yards. Bulkeley was penalized for off-side. Stanley made 8 yards around left end. He almost got away with a clear field but Bradshaw cut in through from the rear and brought him down. Ricketts plunged 5 yards through right guard. Stanley made 5 yards between left end and left tackle. Graham made the necessary 2 yards by plunging 5 yards through right guard. Bulkeley substituted Glenn for Britton. Stanley made 6 yards through right guard and Keefe stole through the line for 5 yards more. Stanley made 15 yards to the goal line, but was brought back to the three yard line for off-sides. The Bulkeley line held like a rock and the Academy backfield couldn't find a hole. Bulkeley captured the ball on downs on their own 2 yard line and NFA was penalized for off-side.

The ball was kicked after Bulkeley had made 10 yards once and had been penalized ten yards for holding. Keefe fumbled the ball before the punt and May got the ball also on a ten-yard start. Keefe, Ricketts and Stanley tore off after him, and stopped him on his little excursion toward the Norwich goal line before he had gone 20 yards. At the end of the first quarter the ball was in Bulkeley's possession on the Academy 30 yard line.

Second Quarter

On the opening of the second quarter Donnelly ploughed 3 yards through right guard. McMillian broke through the line and threw Mallon for a 5 yard loss. The NFA line took a brace and held Bulkeley to downs. The Academy lost the pig-skin on downs by a narrow margin. Bulkeley fumbled and Stanley recovered the ball. May broke through the line and threw Keefe for a loss. Gallup threw Stanley for a loss. Stanley punted to Mallon who fumbled but recovered. Bulkeley was forced to kick. The Academy ran the ball back to the Bulkeley's 40 yard line by plunging and short end runs. Stanley attempted a drop-kick, but his attempt was fruitless.

Third Quarter
Sullivan got the kickoff but was pulled down by Ferguson and McMillian before he could get a good start. Bulkeley made 7 yards by using Donnelly as a ram for line plunging. Although several times Bulkeley only got its distance by a margin of a few inches, the Academy didn't seem to be able to stop them. Bulkeley's attempt to drop kick on the last down from the 25 yard was a miserable failure.

Stanley made two 8-yard runs in succession but the Academy was forced to punt. Reddon was afraid to touch the ball for fear he would fumble it, and waited until Mallon fell on it for him. Bulkeley was unable to gain and lost the ball on downs.

Fourth Quarter

Ricketts opened the quarter with a 7 yard run through tackle. Stanley made 8 yards around left end and 8 yards between end and tackle. The academy used a box formation for an end run and line plunge with some success. A forward pass to Ricketts netted 20 yards. Stanley made 7 yards through the line, and almost broke through Bulkeley's secondary defense. Ricketts made 8 yards around right end. Stanley made the first touchdown by tearing off the necessary 8 yards around the other end. He kicked the goal with perfect accuracy.

Score was 7-0 in favor of the Academy.

Bulkeley received the kick-off but didn't run the kick back 2 yards for both Ferguson and Lynch got down under the kick in good style, and both tackled the runner together. Donnelly was thrown for a 5 yard loss when Lynch brought him down behind his line. On the fourth down Bulkeley attempted a fake punt but was thrown for a 10 yard loss. Lynch was off-side and NFA was penalized 5 yards. Bulkeley kicked to the Academy's 25 yard line.

A forward pass to Keefe netted 25 yards. Keefe ran far out to his right end. The ball was snapped, and thrown obliquely down the field to Keefe. The play was so simple that Bulkeley thought that the Academy was trying to draw its backfield over to the right. A forward pass to Lynch netted 15 yards. Stanley dropped a drop-kick squarely between the goal posts, from the 42 yard line. It was the prettiest kick that Stanley has made this season. Men were leaking through the line and he had to get it away quickly. It is safe to say that Stanley kicked the prettiest field goal that has ever been seen in an Academy-Bulkeley game. The score was 10–0 in favor of the Academy.

Bulkeley was forced to punt, and Stanley ran the kick back 15 yards. The whistle for time out blew just as the Academy was settling into its stride.

The lineup as follows:

NFA		*Bulkeley*
Sears	*Left End*	*Bradshaw*
McMillian	*Left Tackle*	*Gallup*
Senft	*Left Guard*	*May*
Eastwood	*Center*	*Tevlin*
Kozlowski	*Right Guard*	*Britton*
Wilcox	*Right Tackle*	*Lawski*
Parker	*Right End*	*Sullivan*
Keefe	*Quarter Back*	*Mellon*
Ricketts	*Left Half Back*	*Whitcomb*
Graham	*Full Back*	*Redden*
Stanley	*Right Half Back*	*Donnelly*

Referee, Ebbs. Umpire Wholley, Timers Stanley, Ema. Head Linesman, Keefe. Linesmen, Harrington, Hertz.

Substitutes for Bulkeley—Glenn for Britton, O'Neil for Glenn.

Substitutes for NFA—Ferguson for Sears, Lynch for Graham, Donnell for Senft.

The quarters were 12–10 minutes and 12–10 minutes.

It was to be the last win for Norwich in New London for thirteen years.

Season at a Glance: 1917

For the first time, the rivalry was reported as an "ancient" rivalry, one that to this point had lasted forty-two years. Bulkeley had lost three in a row but hosted Norwich on November 3 in better shape. Mistakes from Norwich also contributed to a 14–0 win for the home team. Weaknesses in the center of the NFA line also contributed to victory, as did the apparent lack of spirit from the Norwich side.

The following was printed in the November 5, 1917 edition of the *Bulletin*:

> *The Academy football team lost to its ancient rival, Bulkeley School, of New London, at Plant Field, Saturday for the first time in three years. The Academy defeat was directly traceable to the weakness of the center of the Academy line on both offense and defense. Phillips paved the way for all of Bulkeley's scores by some error. Bulkeley had a stone-wall line and a quartet of line-plunging backs who gained almost at will through the Red and White line between tackle and tackle. The Academy backs did not have a show for if they tried the ends they were nailed from behind while if they tried to hit the line the Bulkeley linemen were through to them before they could reach the line of scrimmage. Mallon quickly recognized that end runs were hopeless methods of gaining with Oat and Counihan and after trying the line once he wisely sent his backs through center and guard. Almost invariably it was the secondary line of defense or one of the tackles who stopped the man. The passing of Phillips to his backs was bad throughout the game but it became especially noticeable on the punt formations when the ball seemed to go anywhere except to Bennett.*
>
> *The Academy showed at its best in the first quarter when they carried the ball down the field to Bulkeley's six-yard line where they were held for downs. Bulkeley's first score came after a blocked kick and then a New London man fell on the ball on NFA's six-yard line. The ball was carried to within six inches of the Academy goal where it was fumbled and when the heap of men was pulled apart the ball was a bone of contention between Oat and a Bulkeley guard. Bulkeley got the ball however and scored on the next play.*
>
> *The second score came in the third quarter when Bennett fumbled a "wild throw" by Phillips and a New London man recovered it. With*

the NFA backs desperately trying to plug the hole at center Mallon threw the ball to Fitch who took two steps for the score. Phillips handed Bulkeley two more points in the fourth quarter to make up for Mallon's missed goals when he passed to Bennett who was forced to fall on the ball behind his own goal line. Eastwood sent Phillips from the field and took center himself, "Al" Henault taking his place at halfback. But like Johnson McGraw in a rather similar case last month, Eastwood was locking the door after the horse had been stolen. True, Bulkeley did not score again, but they did not need to. NFA opened a machine gun attack of forward passes in the last quarter but only one of them worked. One of the prettiest plays of the game was made when Bennett faking a pass ducked under the out-stretched arms of the Bulkeley forwards and made a short run. The reason of the Bulkeley victory was clearly shown as when Eastwood was at center the Bulkeley backs hit the line in vain. The game was of the steady plugging style that failed to show individual stars but the playing of Eastwood, Bennett, Koslowski and Oat for the Academy and Whitcomb, Babbidge, Sullivan and Fitch of Bulkeley was noticeable although perhaps no more praise-deserving than that of other men in the game. Bulkeley was weak in the kicking game and her ends failed to get down under Mallon's punts.

The game was cleanly played and there was no slugging as has marred those games in former years. The Bulkeley cheering squad did not show as good sportsmanship as might be desired when they yelled, "Oh you bums," but perhaps they didn't know any better. The NFA cheering squad was smaller than usual and seemed to lack some of its old time pep. The lighter voices of the girls were much more noticeable than in former years. The NFA special was quiet on the way down to this game, an unheard of thing in former years and is only to be attributed to a falling off of school spirit. Between the halves the Bulkeley supporters did a snake dance on the field while the Norwich rooters sang some of their war songs.

Lineup and summary:

N.F.A.		*Bulkeley*
Oat	*L.E.*	*Fitch*
Tirrell	*L.T.*	*Davis*

Suplicki	*L.G.*	*O'Neil*
Phillips	*C*	*Babbidge*
R. Wilcox	*R.G.*	*Dolbeare*
Koslowski	*R.T.*	*Feeley*
Counihan	*R.E.*	*Sullivan*
Brewer	*Q.B.*	*Mallon (capt.)*
Eastwood (capt,)	*L.H.B.*	*Spicer*
Bennett	*R.H.B.*	*Murphy*
J. Wilcox	*F.B.*	*Whitcomb*

Referee, Steward; umpire, Murray; linesman, French; timers, Hull and Dowhirst; quarters, 12, 10, 12, 10.

Score by Quarters

BHS	*0*	*6*	*6*	*2*
NFA	*0*	*0*	*0*	*0*

Scoring: Touchdowns, Whitcomb, Fitch; missed goals from touchdowns, Mallon 2; substitutes, BHS, none; NFA, Brend for Tirrell, Tirrell for Brend, Eastwood for Phillips, Henault for Eastwood.

Norwich returned with a victory two weeks later, on November 17, at the Academy campus thanks to a trick play. At the start of the game, on a pass play, a Norwich receiver "hid" along the sidelines, raced down the field once the ball was snapped, hauled in the pass and went over for a touchdown.

It was the only touchdown in a 7–2 game. Wrote the *Bulletin* on November 19:

> *One of the Best Games Seen on Campus in Recent Years—Trick Play Big Factor in NFA Score—Bulkeley Gets Safety When NFA Missed Signals—Bulkeley puts Up Big Fight in Last Quarter—Sullivan Individual Star*
>
> *Saturday afternoon the Norwich Free Academy team beat the eleven from Bulkeley School in New London in one of the best football games ever seen here. Both teams played hard, consistent football from start to finish, each team scoring on some fluke. The Academy score came as a direct result of a trick play of the McKay brand, Eastwood getting away for a forty-yard run. Before Bulkeley could fully recover the ball was over the line. Bulkeley's lone two points came in the third quarter when Mallon*

sent a punt to the NFA ten-yard line and then somebody on the Red and White team was too thick to get the signals as the ball was passed to no one in particular. Bennett was a fraction of a second ahead of Sullivan in landing on the ball, thereby depriving Bulkeley of five points. The last quarter started with a rush, the Academy making a couple of good gains and then a blocked kick gave New London the ball. The visiting team took the ball down the field in a series of center bucks and off-tackle plays until the ball was near the twenty-yard line, four rushes netted but nine yards and the Academy protested when Bulkeley kept the ball. The notes of the reporters for both the Bulletin *and the New London paper showed it to be the fifth down but the referee stuck to his decision. The Academy got the ball finally a yard from her goal and was forced to punt. Murphy got the kick by a circus tackle by R. Wilcox. On the last play of the game Eastwood got the ball three inches from the Academy goal.*

The game was fast from the first kick-off until the final whistle, although Bulkeley's play was marred by frequent penalties for offside. All four backs on both teams played great football but the fine plunging of Eastwood and Wilcox of the Academy and the headwork of Captain Mallon of Bulkeley were especially worthy of mention. Bennett proved a dangerous man as did Spicer of Bulkeley. On the line Koslowski and R. Wilcox shone for Norwich while Feeley, although he lost many yards for his team by offside, got some good tackles. Both the Academy ends played brilliant football, Counihan making a good run and breaking up a couple of passes while Oat saved the Academy from a score when he fell on Eastwood's fumble on an intercepted pass. Sullivan of Bulkeley was the individual star of the game as he was a deadly man at the receiving end of a pass, and at the same time broke through many times, and cutting down the Norwich backs.

Bulkeley made several fumbles in the line plunging in the first quarter and Captain Eastwood of the Academy made a couple of muffs that might very easily have turned the tide had it not been for excellent work on the part of his teammates.

NFA	*Bulkeley*	
Oat	*L.E.*	*Fitch*
Tirrell	*L.T.*	*Davis*
Suplicki	*L.G.*	*O'Neil*

Covello		*C*		*Babbidge*
R. Wilcox		*R.G.*		*Dolbeare*
Koslowski		*R.T.*		*Feeley*
Counihan		*R.E.*		*Sullivan*
Brewer		*Q.B.*		*Mallon (capt.)*
Eastwood (capt,)		*L.H.B.*		*Spicer*
Bennett		*R.H.B.*		*Murphy*
J. Wilcox		*F.B.*		*Demosh*
Score By Quarters				
NFA	*7*	*0*	*0*	*0–7*
BHS	*0*	*0*	*2*	*0–2*

Substitutions: NFA, none; BHS, T. Murphy for Delbeare. Referee, Edward Murray, Trinity; Referee, C.J. Sharpe, Colby College. Head linesman, Houlihan, NCS Timers, Alofsin (Norwich) and Yarvots (Bulkeley).

The first game of the 1919 season went to Bulkeley, 12–7. Things seemed to have been going fine for Norwich through the first two quarters, but the *Bulletin* reporter noted:

> *In the third canto, when everything looked rosy, the trouble started. With the Academy in possession of the ball on their 35-yard line and in no apparent danger, old man Hard Luck entered the grounds, took a liking to the Norwich boys and followed them around the rest of the afternoon.*

Bulkeley scored twice in this quarter, the last time on a forward pass:

> *Standing on the NFA 45-yard line, McInnis hurled a long forward pass to Captain Fitch, the rangy right end who jogged thirty yards for a touchdown. Two or three Academy players attempted to tackle him en route but failed. It was a shame to let him get away with it.*

NFA caught some semblance of revenge in the second game two weeks later, playing to a 7–7 tie.

3

BULKELEY GETS NOTICED

1920–1929

Norwich began the first two years of the Roaring Twenties on a high note, going 3-0-1 between 1920 and 1921. But that early dominance ended fast.

The 1922 Bulkeley squad was, for the first time, a force to be reckoned with. All throughout the season, Bulkeley ran roughshod over its opponents, and that came to a head in the November 11 meeting with NFA.

For the first time, Bulkeley and NFA played once in a season, a trend that held for the next fifty-five years. For Norwich, this probably was a good thing after it lost, 44–6, at home. The win clinched an Eastern Connecticut/Western Rhode Island Championship, which was the first incarnation of a conference for the local teams.

The fireworks weren't relegated to just the scoreboard. As the *New London Evening Day* reported on November 13:

> *The game was hard played and rough at times, and the hard spirit of friendly rivalry that has usually attended the annual clashes of the two schools, was marred by the rowdy conduct of a group of Norwich fans, who engaged in a pitched battle with Bulkeley supporters and endeavored to mob the Orange and Black team.*
>
> *Hostilities started on the sidelines after the Academy captain slugged Watterson of the Bulkeley eleven. The Academy leader slammed the*

local boy on the back of the neck, and Watterson turned around and handed the Norwich boy a slam in return. They started to mix things up when play stepped between them, and both were ordered out of the game. Norwich needed the services of their leader, however, and Bulkeley agreed to his getting back into the game, provided the ban was lifted on Watterson. It was so agreed and the incident passed.

For a time it threatened to be a free-for-all, and at the conclusion of the game, a group of New London business men formed a cordon around the local players until police arrived to protect them from assault by the mob. In fact the Bulkeley players had to go to their dressing rooms escorted by the police, who held the unruly mob at bay. To make matters worse, the local players were compelled to wait 20 minutes before they could get their clothes, which were in the locker rooms under lock and key, and the possessor of the key was among the missing.

The bus was driven up to the door of the locker room where the Bulkeley players got aboard and were hastily driven off, with the police keeping the angry rooters and drunks at a distance. Bulkeley authorities plan to have no recurrence of the rowdyism at the local field, when the Academy come to this city for a return game, and plans will be carried out so as to ensure extending the visiting players every courtesy, while order will be assured at the football field with augmented police protection if necessary.

Game at a Glance: November 8, 1924

One year after a 33–0 victory, Bulkeley again added to Norwich's misery with a second 33–0 win in 1924. In front of a large crowd at Norwich, Bulkeley scored early and often en route to the easy win.

The November 10, 1924 *Bulletin* featured the headline "Bulkeley Smashes Through the Academy Team to a 33 to 0 Victory":

Before one of the largest crowds witnessing a game on the Academy campus Saturday afternoon, the Bulkeley High School team overwhelmed the NFA by a score of 33–0.

Bulkeley, aspirants for the state title, began their march to victory in the opening quarter. By continual line plunging they made the first of a series of touchdowns against a weaker and inexperienced, but fighting Norwich eleven.

One thing may be said of the local boys and that is they fought hard for their Alma Mater, but were overcome by a great Bulkeley machine.

The red and white team was no match for the heavier gridiron stars of the Whaling City school and the Bulkeley team ran wild through the Academy defense and immediately checked the local offense before it started.

Bulkeley, despite its overwhelming victory, was not up to the caliber of which it was thought to be. Whether the Orange and Black were too overconfident is not known. The Academy team knowing that they were opposing one of the greatest teams in Connecticut, fought gamely and with determination to hold Bulkeley to a low score. Sportsmanship on both sides were the main issue of the game and the spectators saw many thrilling dashes and plays. Moreover each man on both teams was in the game every minute, trying to add further glory to his school.

The Orange and Black eleven should rejoice in their victory over their traditional rivals, whom they have only been able to overcome in the past few seasons. The state title is their aim and this should be easy to attain after their spectacular playing Saturday.

The Academy is not disheartened in their defeat. As they know that they have held a great team to a score which followers thought would only be a fraction of what it really was.

Captain Sheflott, Rice, Daniels and Henkle starred for the Bulkeley eleven. Rice by his open field running was a real Red Grange. Henkle came into the limelight by making of the longest runs ever seen on a high school gridiron.

For the Academy, Henrichs, Higgins and Williams were the outstanding backfield players and Carlin, Lukoski and Hollander distinguished themselves on the line.

GAME BY QUARTERS

First quarter—Hinrichs of the Academy kicked off the Bulkeley. Ball went behind the posts and was brought to play on the 20 yard line.

Bulkeley then started a march up the field making six consecutive first downs. Rice took the ball over for the first touchdown. Rice succeeded in a try for point. Daniels, of Bulkeley, kicked off to the Academy. It was the Academy's ball on her 20 yard line. On the next play an Academy back fumbled the ball and it was recovered by graves of Bulkeley on the 20 yard line. Bulkeley was penalized 5 yards for offsides. Bulkeley made two attempts by forward passes, but these were incomplete. Bulkeley lost the ball after four tries to gain Academy's ball on the 15-yard line. A forward pass, Williams to Carlin, netted first down for the Academy. Here the Bulkeley line held and Hinrichs of the Academy kicked on the fourth down. Henkle caught the ball on the 10 yard line and ran it back 5 yards. Quarter ended here with the ball in Bulkeley's possession on her 15 yard line.

Second quarter: Bulkeley completed a long forward to Sheflott that went for a touchdown. However this score did not count and Bulkeley was penalized 15 yards for having a player hiding on the sidelines. Bulkeley was forced to knick on her fourth down. Academy's ball on her 20 yard line. Academy could not get through for any gains and was compelled to kick on the fourth down. Bulkeley's ball on her 39 yard line. After four line plunges Bulkeley made first down. Rice ran the remaining distance for a touchdown. Rice succeeded a try for point. Daniels of Bulkeley kicked off to the Academy. Hinrichs received the ball on the 3-yard line and brought it back 20 yards. Academy was penalized 5 yards for offside. Bulkeley's line was a stonewall and the Academy making no gains kicked on its fourth down. Bulkeley's ball on the 45-yard line. Bulkeley made first down. Bulkeley was penalized 15 yards for slugging. Bulkeley's ball on her 30-yard line. Daniels completed a forward netting 40 yards. Rice ran the remaining distance for a touchdown and succeeded in a try for point. Daniels of Bulkeley kicked off to Academy. Higgins received the ball on the 10-yard line and ran it back 10 yards. Half ended at this point.

Third quarter: Henrichs of Academy kicked off to Henkle of Bulkeley, who made a sensational run of 35 yards for a touchdown. Rice failed in a try for point. Bulkeley kicked off to Academy. MacGowan caught the ball on the 3-yard line and ran it back 17 yards. Academy failed to make first down and surrendered the ball to Bulkeley on her 29-yard line. Bulkeley tried two passes, both being incomplete. Another forward, Henkle to Daniels, netted 20 yards and first down. Rice took the ball over again for a touchdown, but failed in a try for point. Bulkeley kicked to Academy. The Academy man who received the ball fumbled and Bulkeley covered it on the 20-yard line. Bulkeley for the second time in the game was penalized 15 yards for slugging. Henkle of Bulkeley fumbled the ball and it was recovered by Higgins on the 27-yard line. Bulkeley line held here and the Academy kicked on its fourth down. Henkle received the ball on the 50 yard line and ran it back 20 yards. Bulkeley lost the ball after four attempts to get through and it was the Academy's ball on the 13-yard line. Carlin caught a forward pass netting first down for the Academy. Quarter ended with the Academy having the ball on the 23-yard line.

Fourth quarter: A forward pass, Williams to Hinrichs, netted first down. Hinrichs of Academy kicked on fourth down. Bulkeley's ball on the 56-yard line. Bulkeley made three successive first downs. Dunn of the Academy went in for Polsky. Bulkeley made another first down. Academy holds Bulkeley for four downs on the 5-yard line. Carpentier of Academy went in for Higgins. Hinrichs kicked the ball on the fourth down to Bulkeley. Bulkeley made first down. Here the Academy's line held and it was the Academy's ball on her 7-yard line. Hinrichs on the next play kicked the ball to Bulkeley. Bulkeley's ball on the 34-yard line. Holdridge of Academy went in for MacGowan. Rice went though for first down. Game ended here.

NFA		*Bulkeley*
Hollander	*L.E.*	*Graves*
Lukowski	*L.T.*	*Gavett*
Polsky	*L.G.*	*Wilson*
Haslam (Capt.)	*C*	*Dillon*
Stefano	*R.G.*	*Brown*
Scott	*R.T.*	*Watterson*
Carlin	*R.E.*	*Daniels*
Williams	*Q.B.*	*Henkle*
Higgins	*L.H.B.*	*Rice*

Above: The 1928 NFA team. NFA beat Bulkeley 18–0 in 1928.

Right: The 1927 Bulkeley team tied NFA 6–6.

MacGowan	*R.H.B.*	*Sheflott (Capt.)*
Hinrichs	*F.B.*	*Collins*

Referee, Durgin of the Sub Base. Field umpire, Brigham. Time keeper, MacNamara. Head linesman, Hull. Time of quarters, 12 minutes.

Score by Quarters

BHS	*7*	*14*	*12*	*0–33*
NFA	*0*	*0*	*0*	*0–0*

Bulkeley continued its dominance in 1925, winning 13–12. But NFA got some measure of revenge in 1926, scoring a 6–0 win in front of approximately five thousand fans on the Academy campus.

The teams tied, 6–6, in 1927, before NFA won the 1928 contest, 18–0. That win carried over to the next year, when the Wildcats—adopted as the team's mascot by this point (Bulkeley had chosen the Tigers)—continued their winning ways but at a place that hadn't seen much luck.

Game at a Glance: November 23, 1929

By this sixty-sixth meeting between the teams, Bulkeley had moved its home games to Mercer Field, which was situated between Bank Street and Willets Avenue. The field was named for Frederic Mercer, a local supporter of athletics.

Norwich was still looking for its first victory in New London during the 1920s. All it took was a third-quarter touchdown from Frank (Gink) Barber to seal the win for the Wildcats.

The following is from the Monday, November 25 edition of the *New London Evening Day*:

Mercer Field, Bulkeley's home for many years from the 1920s through the 1950s.

New London, Nov. 23—Breaking a jinx that had extended back to 1916, Norwich Free Academy's Wildcats smashed through to a 7 to 0 victory over the Bulkeley Tigers in its home lair at Mercer field Saturday afternoon in their 66th meeting. The last NFA football win in New London had been achieved just 13 years ago.

Taking advantage of their one real break of the game, the Academy boys scored in the middle of the third quarter after blocking a kick and recovering it deep in their rival's territory. Frank (Gink) Barber, who has been the mainstay of the eleven all year, finally crashed over for the score and the extra point was converted by Golembeskie diving over the line.

Les Crowell Outstanding Player

While it fell to the lot of Barber to score the touchdown the outstanding player for the Academy cause, the one who gave Bulkeley piles of trouble all afternoon, was Les Crowell, the right tackle. It was he who recovered the blocked kick that gave the Wildcats their scoring chance and it was he who broke through repeatedly to throw the Orange and Black runners for losses. Crowell also did the kicking for the first half of the game and easily outdistanced his Bulkeley rival the major part of the time. Sharing the honors with Cromwell were Ed Flather, left end; Hertz, left tackle; Barber and Brewer in the backfield.

Capt. Ken Barrows, end, and Pat Halifteras, halfback, gained the most ground for Bulkeley with some beautiful catches of forward passes. Collins and DeGaetano, in the backfield, also played well.

Bulkeley threw away four distinct chances to score, once in the second quarter when a Tiger punt was grounded on the 3-yard line and the Academy's return kick was short; and three times in the last quarter when they battled within the ten-yard line only to be hurled back from the promised land.

On the fourth try, however, it was the umpire's whistle that called a halt for the game ended with Bulkeley in possession of the ball on the Academy's two-yard line, with one more down to make it.

NFA MAKES DESPERATE STANDS

These four goal-line stands by the Academy may either be classed as great work by the NFA forwards or dumb playing by the Bulkeley backfield. It was probably a combination of both, for the Academy was charging in fast and Bulkeley was fumbling or slow with their runs when things became tight.

Working a baffling forward-passing game, Bulkeley had the Academy worried all through the second half and particularly the last quarter. It was these passes that put them within the ten-yard line on four occasions, when the ends and halfbacks and particularly Barrows and Halifteras were left uncovered time and again. The Academy had no defense for this manner of play.

Play was in Academy territory for the greater part of the game but the Academy was not outplayed that bad. Bulkeley, however, made ten first downs to the Academy's five. Poor kicks in two instances gave Bulkeley their chances to get past the 50-yard line and up in the shadows of the Wildcat posts. Neither team had any offense to speak of, outside of Bulkeley passing proclivities. The Academy had no particular play with which it could gain consistently.

ACADEMY SECONDS START GAME

Coach Whitney started his second Norwich team. Bulkeley received the opening kickoff on its 10-yard line, running it out to the 35-yard marker. Bulkeley kicked on third down to the Academy 40-yard line. The academy made one first down, a 10-yard run by Zigstoriak. The Academy lost the ball on downs on Bulkeley's 35-yard line and Bulkeley punted back to the NFA 30-yard stripe.

On the first play, the Academy fumbled and recovered and here the Academy first team made its appearance. On the next down the Wildcats punted to midfield and Bulkeley kicked on fourth down to the 20-yard line. The Academy punted back to midfield as the quarter ended with Bulkeley in possession of the ball on the Academy 45-yard line.

Bulkeley got its first break in the early part of the second quarter when a punt was grounded on the NFA 3-yard line. The Academy got off a short punt that went to the 20-yard marker. Bulkeley smashed through to a first down on the nine yard line but a forward pass was grounded over the goal line on fourth down after Bulkeley had lost three yards on three plays and the Academy took the ball on their 20-yard line.

The Academy, for some reason or other, essayed to pass from their 20-yard line and Fontaine's toss went right into the hands of a Bulkeley man on the 30-yard stripe. This was another break.

Academy Complete Only One Pass

Bulkeley reeled off a first down to come within the 20-yard line but Flather intercepted a pass and almost got away free. Barber and Fontaine collaborated for a first down and then Fontaine made one all alone with a 12-yard run to the 40-yard line. Fontaine tossed a pass to Barber on Bulkeley's 40-yard line but the half ended to stop this short spurt of the Red and White. This, by the way, was the only pass completed by the Academy all day.

Bulkeley received again in the second half on their 25-yard line and made a short gain. A pass to DeGaetano made the distance to midfield but Bulkeley was unable to gain and decided to kick.

Crowell Recovers Kick

The pass came back true from center, the kick's foot was set to meet the pigskin, but lo and behold, it seemed like the whole left side of the Academy line, Hertz and Wojstasiak, anyway, rushed in upon the kick. The ball struck one of them and bounded back about 20 or 30 yards. Cruickshank, center, and Crowell were after it. Cruickshank made an attempt to pick it up but instead, booted it on towards the goal and Crowell finally fell on it on the 14-yard line.

The Academy tried two line plays that gained but little. Fontaine dropped back to pass but seeing no one to receive the ball, ran down along the sidelines before being forced outside at the 3-yard line for a first down. Barber then took it over on second down, crashing through the right side of the Bulkeley line. When the extra point was converted, Academy rooters went even a little wilder than they had a moment before.

Bulkeley received the kickoff and staged a little offensive show bringing the ball to the Academy 40-yard line, with three first downs and then punted just as the quarter ended.

BULKELEY THREATENS CONTINUALLY

The last quarter saw Bulkeley make several threatening gestures at putting over a score but always lacked the final punch. The Academy punted back to midfield at the start of the quarter. DeGaetano ran around end for 20 yards, bringing the ball to the 30-yard line. A pass to Barrows brought the ball to the nine yard line and Berghinzo, on fourth down, intercepted a pass on his three yard line after Bulkeley had failed to gain by line plays. The Academy punted out to their 30-yard line and again Bulkeley uncorked a neat pass, this time to Halifteras, that brought the ball to the 10-yard line. Still again, Bulkeley could not gain after four downs and lost the ball when a pass was grounded over the goal line.

Stevens got off a short kick that went offside at the 30-yard line after the ball had been brought out to the 20-yard marker. Bulkeley for the last time, again started towards the touchdown that never came. A pass to the ten-yard line, held twice, a slice by Aguiar, who had just been inserted to the 3-yard line—and then the whistle. The game was over.

Summary:

NFA		*Bulkeley*
Mullins	*L.E.*	*Little*
Hayden	*L.T.*	*Luck*
Abugle	*L.G.*	*Eilon*
Mack	*C*	*Johnson*
Kirstein	*R.G.*	*Smith*
Cote	*R.T.*	*Dean*
Berkman	*R.E.*	*Barrows*
Zigstoriak	*Q.B.*	*Rockwell*
Cotter	*L.H.B.*	*DeGaetano*
Golembeskie	*R.H.B.*	*Halifteras*
Geer	*F.B.*	*Collins*

Score

NFA	*0*	*0*	*7*	*0–7*
BHS	*0*	*0*	*0*	*0–0*

Touchdown—Barber; points after touchdown, Golembeskie (rush). Referee, Parker; umpire, McGrath; head linesman, O'Loughlin. Time, 10-minute quarters.

4
NFA FIGHTS BACK
1930–1939

By 1930, Bulkeley had a new rival on its schedule: Chapman Tech. The vocational school, also located in New London, featured an opportunity for brothers to play against brothers, which happened often. Tech was a worthy adversary; the Huskies went 8-0 in 1933 to win the Waskowitz Trophy.

Still, the Tigers had their rival to the north: Norwich. The 1929 win for NFA was one of the final good vibes the team felt for some time. From 1930 to 1933, Bulkeley outscored the Wildcats, 59–0.

One of the first great players for Bulkeley was Pericles (Pat) Haleftiras. A halfback, Haleftiras scored the only touchdown in a 6–0 win in the November 22, 1930 game. Tied at 0–0 at the half, Bulkeley reeled off sixty-five yards in three plays, the last coming on Haleftiras's eight-yard run, in front of 2,500 fans in Norwich.

Bulkeley made it a winning streak with a 28–0 win on November 21, 1931. The win clinched the Eastern Connecticut/Western Rhode Island Championship for the first time in nine years. Haleftiras and Ernie Brooks scored touchdowns, and Joe Murphy drop-kicked two extra points. "'Dutch' Cote, a 220-pound tackle, and diminutive 'Stephie' Stepham were the outstanding Wildcats," wrote the *New London Evening Day*.

Heavy rains contributed to a low-scoring affair on November 19, 1932. Only 1,100 fans showed up to the game that was played in a quagmire.

The 1931 Bulkeley team shut out NFA, 28–0, for its second straight shutout in the rivalry.

The 1932 Bulkeley team needed just one touchdown to beat NFA 6–0.

According to the *New London Evening Day*, "So deep was the water on the field that the players several times took advantage of it and washed the mud from their faces and hands in one of the puddles."

Still, the weather didn't faze Bulkeley's Ed Kurpiewski. He reeled off a ninety-nine-yard run, the longest in the rivalry's history, and it came late in the second quarter, according to the *Day*:

> *The run came as the result of a punt in the second quarter with but four minutes left to play. The Wildcats were forced to punt after all attempts to gain by line plays failed. The punt sailed over the head of Charlie Messer, Bulkeley quarterback, who at the time was playing in the safety position. The ball rolled to the Bulkeley one yard line. While Norwich men waited for it to roll still nearer the goal line before downing it, Kurpiewski came up from the behind, seized the pigskin and before any of the Wildcat men could touch him was off for the sidelines. Interference immediately formed for him and cleared the way while Kurpiewski raced through the rain and mud to a touchdown.*

The 1933 NFA team. Bulkeley shut out the 1933 NFA team for the fourth straight year.

Bulkeley made it four in a row on November 25, 1933, when Kurpiewski scored two more touchdowns and James Logioco added the other in a 19–0 win. But of more importance was that the Tigers claimed an "unofficial mascot," according to the *Day*:

> *It appears as though the Tigers have a mascot. At least, Ernie Hamilton, substitute quarterback, had a hard time chasing his dog off the field. The incident caused a great deal of laughter from the crowd. Incidentally, Susie, as the team calls Ernie's dog, has yet to miss a Bulkeley practice session. When signal drill goes to slow, Coaches O'Brien and Balentine send Susie after those loafing and a couple of sharp molars give her complete command over the boys.*

Norwich, though, put its losing streak to an end in a big way the following year. Featuring players such as Raymond "Pop" Congdon, a tackle and kicker who played three sports, and Charlie Rudak, a fullback and leading rusher, NFA ran roughshod over its opponents. Head coach Paul Bitgood worked with the linemen, and assistant

The 1934 NFA team. NFA completed its turnaround by beating Bulkeley 21–7.

Jimmy Williams, who later would be head coach for a number of years, worked with the backfield.

The Wildcats opened the season with a 19–7 win over Manchester and then proceeded to outscore its opponents, 146–33, to win the first of six Eastern Connecticut/Western Rhode Island Championships. It shut out Chapman Tech, Fitch and Stonington by identical 14–0 scores and also beat Plainfield, 29–0. Additional wins over Westerly (21–12) and Windham (14–7) set up the final game against its familiar rival.

On November 17, 1934, the Wildcats scored twenty-one points in the first half against Bulkeley and hung on for a 21–7 victory. More than five thousand fans jammed the Academy field, which Norwich authorities placed as one of the largest crowds to witness a football game at their field. Jack MacKay (twice) and Bill Fitzgerald scored two touchdowns for the Wildcats, and John (Scotty) Thompson tallied for Bulkeley.

NFA finished the season 8-0. At the time, there was no official state championship. A game was set up the following week against New Britain, which finished 9-0. Bad weather, however, canceled the game.

In 1984, the *Norwich Bulletin* ran an article on the fiftieth anniversary of one of the best seasons to date:

> *Bitgood, in a letter to surviving members, tells how one player "had a severely bruised leg that was black and blue from knee to ankle. A sorry sight to view. He borrowed one of his mother's coffee pots, and in the manual training department of the school, fashioned a protective device to be strapped on his leg…*
>
> *This was covered with felt, both inside and out, to pass the judgment of the officials. He played with it until it healed. Another one with a severly bruised shoulder fashioned sort of a bridge device that when placed underneath his shoulder pads, would protect the shoulder when blocking or tackling…Such a fundamental spirit was shown by the whole group.*
>
> *John Moore, a center and guard and the captain in 1934, recalled the Bulkeley game, which marked the continuation of the nation's oldest high school football rivalry, begun in 1875.*
>
> *"Actually, the entire season was our last game with Bulkeley of New London," said Moore, who is treasurer of Norwich. "I remember*

> *we had them 21–0 and myself and a couple of others begged the quarterback (Jack MacKay) to throw so we could get one more score. Well, he threw and a guy intercepted it and ran it back about 88 yards for a touchdown."*

Norwich continued its winning ways with a thrilling 9–6 win on November 16, 1935, in front of 2,500 at Mercer Field.

Matthew LaBonte scored a touchdown, and Joe Butova kicked an extra point in the second quarter to give NFA a 7–0 lead going into halftime.

Albo Secchiaroli scored a touchdown in the third quarter for Bulkeley, but the extra point missed. Secchiaroli then contributed to the final points when he was tackled "by the entire Norwich line" in the fourth quarter for a safety. Bulkeley had one last chance but only got as far as the Norwich nineteen-yard line before the final whistle sounded.

Wrote the *New London Day*:

> *There was the usual goal post battle following the game as Norwich rooters attempted to carry away the Mercer field goal posts as souvenirs. Whatever rowdyism occurred at this time was no fault of the students or players of both teams as outsiders seemed more interested in this form of vandalism and took the more active part.*
>
> *During those final minutes, the Tiger star (Secchiaroli) was in a state of near collapse. The Norwich linemen were tackling him viciously and teammates were helping him to his feet after every play. Three plays before the end of the game, co-captain Bill Donovan attempted to lead the exhausted player from the field, but he stubbornly refused and carried on to throw two successful passes to Enrico Uguccioni.*

Game at a Glance: November 19, 1938

The Wildcats continued with victories in 1936 (21–7) and 1937 (19–0), setting up one of the great three-year spans in its history. Two of the greatest players in Norwich history—lineman Gil Bouley and halfback Charlie Weiss—shined in the final two games.

The 1936 Bulkeley-NFA game. NFA eked out a 12–7 win over Bulkeley in 1936.

In 1938, Weiss, a junior, scored two touchdowns as the Wildcats won, 19–0. After the game, Weiss would pick up the first of two straight Player of the Year awards from the *New Haven Register*.

John K. Balentine of the *New London Day* wrote of the game:

> *Norwich Free Academy power was too much for the Bulkeley Tigers in Norwich Saturday afternoon, and the Wildcats romped off with a 19–0 decision as 2,100 fans looked on at the campus gridiron.*
>
> *In winning this 74th football battle between elevens representing the schools, the Academy continued its five-year period of football domination over schools in the Eastern Connecticut Conference. Bulkeley was the last league representative to defeat the Red and White, turning the trick, 19–0, in the final game of the 1933 season.*
>
> *In spite of the heavy rains which preceded the contest, and the intermittent showers during the game, athletes and spectators alike suffered little from the unpleasant conditions. The Norwich gridiron was in excellent shape for the gray, and a loud-speaking system installed in the press box revealed the plays so accurately that fans were able to follow the movements of the players with ease. The rain did, however, remove some of the traditional color connected with the game as student bands were conspicuous by their absence.*
>
> *Contrasting Styles of Play*
>
> *The two elevens offered striking contrasts in their type of attack. Bulkeley, able to net but 11 yards from scrimmage in practically disregarding any attempt to gain via running plays, went into the air 23 times and made*

good 11 tosses to net a gain of 92 yards in this manner. Norwich, with a powerful running game that piled up 280 yards from scrimmage, did not attempt a single aerial.

Although Norwich scored before the contest was three minutes old and appeared to have the situation well in hand throughout, Bulkeley's gallant band of men did come up with one definite scoring threat that threw some scare into Norwich's ranks and caused brief doubt as to the ultimate outcome.

Tigers Miss by Inches

This Bulkeley gesture came in the final period and was a brilliant individual performance on the part of Co-Captain Joseph Podzaline who played the finest game of his career. Starting on the Norwich 43-yard stripe where he recovered a Wildcat fumble, Podzaline figured in 12 of 13 plays that drove inches from the Red and White goal where the advance was checked when a fourth down aerial fell harmlessly in the end zone. In that march, Podzaline passed the ball seven times, connecting with receivers on three occasions to eat up 25 yards, and carried the ball on the other five tries.

Bulkeley's only other advance into Norwich territory, shortly afterwards, resulted in disaster as Edward Lukowski, Norwich guard, intercepted a pass on his own 33-yard line and raced 67 yards for a touchdown.

Weiss Is Standout

Although Podzaline stood head and shoulders above his mates, his bid for individual honors was surpassed by Charles Weiss, 190-pound Norwich fullback. This Norwich ace scored two of his eleven's three touchdowns and was practically impossible to stop. Weiss carried the ball 23 times and picked up 161 yards for his efforts to wind up the fray with an average of seven yards gained per try. Time after time Weiss carried on after his blockers had been removed from the play and on most occasions it took two or even three Bulkeley defenders to bring him down. Ironically enough it was Weiss himself who checked a Norwich advance when he fumbled on the Bulkeley 15-yard line, but other than that the

Wildcat star played perfect football and proved that he is worthy of the title of the outstanding schoolboy player in the state.

Score in First 8 Plays

Norwich broke the ice eight plays after the initial kick off. John Perry kicked poorly to the Red and White 44-yard line and a five-yard return gave Coach Jimmy Williams' boys possession just short of midfield. Weiss lugged the leather five times in the scoring series of plays, climaxing the drive with a 14-yard dash around his left end for the score. Again in the second period the Wildcats tallied after a 53-yard march. Weiss again scored after a four-yard jaunt on a play identical to the one which resulted in the first touchdown.

Bulkeley's touchdown threat, Lukowski's 67-yard run and a Norwich drive that was halted by Weiss' fumble on the Bulkeley 15 were the only features of the second half. Late in the game with the Wildcats leading 19–0, both coaches substituted freely so that boys could get credit toward their varsity letters.

In addition to Podzaline, Bulkeley had other stars. George Chappell added his name to a list of great Bulkeley pass receivers as he offered the chief threat at the end of the Tiger aerial display. Chappell used his height to advantage and frequently outjumped his opponents to capture the ball after near impossible tries. Bernard Wolfe, surprise starter at quarterback, justified his choice by turning in a grand defensive game. Along the line Tom Donovan, center, and Wilfred Benoit, guard, were fighting their way through the steady line of Norwich blockers to make deadly tackles.

Weiss and Lukowski, Norwich stars, received ample support from Acting Captain Henry Butova, who led the Norwich blockers, and Pete Przekop, lineman who practically stopped the Tigers singlehanded when they were only inches from the Red and White goal in the fourth period.

One More Game for NFA

For Bulkeley it was the final game of the year and gave the team a record of four wins, two defeats and one tie as they share the conference title with Stonington. Norwich, with seven wins and a sole defeat, winds up its campaign Thanksgiving day in Norwich against Stamford.

BULKELEY	*NORWICH*
LE-Chappell	*D. Aubrey*
LT-Perry	*Waterman*
LG-Benoit	*Quarto*
C-Donovan	*Leone*
RG-Williams	*Lukowski*
RT-Butleman	*Antonelli*
RE-Hughes	*R. Aubrey*
QB-Wolfe	*Butova*
LHB-Leary	*Ceroone*
RHB-Henderson	*Strickland*
FB-Podzaline	*Weiss*

Norwich	*6*	*7*	*0*	*6–19*

Touchdowns—Weiss 2, Lukowski. Points after touchdown—Butova (placement). Missed points after touchdowns—Butova 2 (placements). Substitutions, Bulkeley—Ballman, Gerity, Clark, Silverstein, Rhea, Dondero, Caldwell, Mosely, Carlson, Gaffney, Dunmire, Hansen, Beers. Norwich—Nowadzadko, Bouley, Przekop, Morosky, Herma, Greiner, Pilling, Barbarossa, DeSoisioio, Hart.

Referee, John McGrath; umpire, Randy Whaples; head linesman, Owen White.

Statistics of the game:

Bulkeley		*Norwich*
11	*yards gained scrimmage*	*280*
6	*first downs*	*11*
23	*passes attempted*	*0*
11	*passes completed*	*0*
92	*yards gained passes*	*0*
0	*passes intercepted by*	*1*
2	*lateral passes*	*0*
3	*yards gained laterals*	*0*
0	*yards penalized*	*60*
3	*number punts*	*4*
44	*average punts*	*36*
2	*fumbles*	*2*
1	*own fumbles recovered*	*1*

As if to make sure that game wasn't a fluke, Weiss—who was referred to as "any man's choice for the all-state fullback position"—scored a touchdown, as did Dick Buckley, in a 12–0 win on November 18, 1939. Wrote the *Day:*

> *Weiss was the whole show offensively for the victors, being the only consistent round gaining back. He carried the ball on sweeps, bucks and off-tackle plays, passed and did the kicking and also backed up the strong side of the line in fine fashion. Gil Bouley was an outstanding lineman at tackle and Pirozek was outstanding on a pass defender.*

The game drew 3,157 to Mercer Field. Frederic W. Mercer, donor of the field, presented the game football to the rival captains: Gil Bouley of

NFA's Gil Bouley was one of the first stars to come out of NFA. He starred at Boston College before a career with the Rams.

Norwich and George Chappell and John Williams of Bulkeley. Jimmy Williams, Norwich coach, was given the football after the game.

In 2000, the *Norwich Bulletin* selected Gil Bouley as one of its top five Eastern Connecticut Athletes of the Century across any sport. Bouley went on to play for Boston College and, after a stellar collegiate career, became the first Norwich athlete to play in the NFL. He spent six seasons as an offensive lineman for the Cleveland/Los Angeles Rams.

5

CHAMPIONSHIPS ABOUND

1940–1949

Norwich began the 1940s just as it left off the 1930s—with a win over Bulkeley. Little did the Wildcats know at the time, but these would be the final good feelings against the Tigers for a while. In fact, the entire state was about to stand up and take notice of Bulkeley.

But first came the November 23, 1940 game on the Academy grounds. Bulkeley's Bob Rockholz and NFA's Alex Avdevich scored first-quarter touchdowns, and the game stood at 6–6 until the final quarter. That's when Lou Caprilozzi stepped up in one of his biggest games as a Wildcat.

The *New London Evening Day* reported:

> *Caprilozzi started the parade with a 10-yard jaunt around the Bulkeley right wing and after a pass from Quarterback Leonard Duff to Right End Carl Nafie, netted 19 yards and a first down on the Orange and Black five, Caprilozzi scored on the final down to win the ball game. The scoring play covered only two yards, but it was the result of Caprilozzi's tremendous driving power since it appeared as though the Bengals had stopped the Norwich ace two yards behind the scrimmage line.*

Norwich's win was its seventh in a row over Bulkeley, but that all came crashing down the following season.

The 1940 Bulkeley–NFA game. NFA's 13–6 win was the seventh in a row for the Wildcats.

Game at a Glance: November 15, 1941

The Waskowitz Trophy was named for a Hartford lawyer and New Britain native, S. Polk Waskowitz, who was born in 1898 and died in July 1933.

The state's sportswriters voted on the top team in the state a few weeks after the season ended, and the winner received this tall trophy. Chapman Tech, Bulkeley's neighbor, was the first recipient of this award in 1933.

Naturally, because of certain loyalties, the award was constantly under scrutiny. New Britain, for example, won the award ten times and Stamford six times, and the most after that was two.

Bulkeley was one of those teams that won two trophies, and the first came in 1941. The Tigers, under the guidance of Bill O'Brien, featured a number of stellar players, starting with co-captains Martin Sheedy (right guard) and Daniel Crowley (left end). Crowley was an all-conference pick, as was left tackle Robert Voight.

Quarterback Joseph Gorra also was a co-captain elect, as was left halfback Robert Rockholz. The duo was named all-conference, and Rockholz was an all-state pick.

The 1941 NFA team was shut out, 40–0, in the game against a superior Bulkeley team that won the Waskowitz Trophy.

It was Keith Johnson, the right halfback, who stood tall in the November 15, 1941 game against Norwich. Three weeks before Japan attacked Pearl Harbor, Bulkeley looked to complete its season undefeated and completed it in a big way.

Written under the headline "Bulkeley Routs Norwich, 40–0, to Virtually Win State Football Title," the *New London Evening Day* reported the following:

> *Bulkeley school's gallant and powerful football machine established itself as the No. 1 team for the Waskowitz trophy, emblematic of the state schoolboy crown, by crushing its arch rival, Norwich Free academy, 40–0, Saturday afternoon at Mercer field to wind up the eight-game slate without a loss or tie.*
>
> *A crowd of 3,587 paying customers, a record for a Bulkeley-Norwich crowd in this city, sat almost spellbound as the charges of Coach Bill O'Brien ran up and down Mercer field with brilliant displays of power and deception to hand the Wildcats their worst football defeat in a score of years and bring the local school its first win over Norwich since 1933.*
>
> *Win Eastern Conn. Crown*
>
> *The victory officially added the eastern Connecticut crown to the Eastern Connecticut conference the Tigers had already won this year, but a final decision on the state championship will be awaited anxiously as the committee to award the trophy will not meet until December.*
>
> *Bulkeley's win assured the team of the highest point rating of any school in the state but there is still some question whether the award*

committee will turn the title over to Bulkeley, a Group B team, instead of a Group A team. The point system of rating was instituted last year when New Britain, a Group A team, had the best percentage in the state. Consequently, this year will bring about the first test of a Group A and Group B rating in quest of the award. New Britain again leads the Group A field but cannot overhaul the Tigers in the point column even if it defeats Hartford Bulkeley Thursday.

TIGERS BLOCKING DEADLY

It is difficult to pick out any Bulkeley star in Saturday's game, since so many factors appeared in the success of the team. The blocking was deadly and the backs thus got away for sensational runs. The passing and kicking were better than usual and the line play defensively was so excellent that Norwich failed to get a single first down against the Bulkeley first stringers.

For sheer brilliance and spectacular play, however, Keith Johnson, one of the best running backs in the state, stood far out in the limelight. Johnson made touchdown runs of 75, 50 and 17 yards, added other sprints ranging from ten to 40 yards and intercepted two Norwich passes. It was his 50-yard touchdown jaunt which started the rout midway in the first period.

GORRA AND KURPIEWSKI STAR

Joe Gorra blocked and directed the team like an All-State performer and was as effective with his duties as Johnson was with his running. Kurpiewski plunged harder Saturday than ever before, and was threat enough to keep the Norwich defense tight and make it easier for the other lads to skirt the ends and riddle the Norwich secondary with aerials.

From wing to wing every Bulkeley lineman was letter perfect. Co-Capt. Dan Crowley and Reggie Eccleston kept Wildcat plays turned inside where bob Voight and Italor Chiapperini made tackle after tackle. Ray Peabody, Co-Capt. Martin Sheedy and Martin Gottestein guarded every inch of the center territory and Joe Murray backed up the line like a Mel Hein.

Lose Score on Fumble

An indication of what was going to happen developed the very first time Bulkeley got the ball when the boys marched 70 yards to the Norwich one-foot line where a fumble gave the Wildcats possession. The Academy immediately punted one but on the second play from scrimmage Johnson dashed 50 yards around his left end for the first touchdown and Bob Rockholz converted.

In the second period the rout was on in earnest as Bulkeley scored three times. The Tigers got possession following a Norwich punt on the visitors' 40-yard line. Two plays netted a first down on the 30 and Johnson then took a reverse to the nine. On fourth down Rockholz hit right tackle for the score and then added the placement.

Two Plays Cover 99 Yards

The next Bulkeley touchdown was the most spectacular of the season. After being forced back to the one yard line on a clipping penalty, Bulkeley struck again and in two plays covered 99 yards. Rockholz ran 24 yards from punt formation on the first attempt and Johnson then cut away behind perfect blocking to dash the remaining 75 on a straight off-tackle thrust. Tom Dorsey added the point as Rockholz was injured on the touchdown play and left the game. The Tiger triple-threat ace was not seriously hurt, however, and will be ready for practice Wednesday when the boys start preparations for the post-season game against Nashua, N.H., on Nov. 27.

Gorra Completes Passes

Shortly after Bulkeley again got the ball at midfield and Gorra tossed three successive passes for a touchdown. The first went to Crowley and covered 15 yards, the next went to Bob Daniels and put the ball on the eight-yard line and the final one was good to Crowley in the end zone.

In the third period Johnson climaxed another 50-yard march with a 17-yard dash for a score and then a jayvee combination of Jack Porter and Bill Ealahan teamed to work a flat pass which netted 25 more yards and the final score. Porter, a freshman, played a goodly part of the game and showed to advantage while Ealahan distinguished himself by sidestepping his way to a touchdown after apparently being trapped by Norwich defenders on several occasions.

NORWICH HELPLESS

While all this Bulkeley power and deception was showing itself Norwich was helpless offensively as well as defensively. Late in the game the Rose City lads marched to the Bulkeley 12 against the third team but at this point the varsity players begged Coach O'Brien to send them back, and when this was done the drive stopped then and there. At the end of the game Bulkeley was deep in Norwich territory and headed for another score.

PLAYERS DUCK COACHES

After the game mild outbursts kept the police active at the ball park as rooters of both elevens interpreted fighting spirit too literally. Outside of a few black eyes and gory noses no harm was done. In the midst of these festivities the Bulkeley team swarmed down from the field house and lifted coach O'Brien up bodily and deposited him in the showers, clothes and all. This traditional bit being completed, the boys then extended the same treatment to Assistant Coaches Pat Haleftiras and Bill Downnie and Faculty Athletic Manager John K. Balentine. The lineups:

BULKELEY

LE, Crowley, Henderson; LT, Chiapperini, F. Johnson, Weigle; LG, Peabody, Mackay, Gottestein; C, Murray, Dunn, Maginniss; RG, Sheedy, Genaros, Ryan, O'Connell; RT, Voight, Schaller; RE, Eccleston, Connors, Flannery; QB, Gorra, Manwaring, Ealahan; LHB, Rockholz, Daniels, Porter; RHB, K. Johnson, Manwaring; FB, Kurpiewski, Davidson.

NORWICH

LE, Killeen, Gilbert, Bromley; LT, Alexopoulos, Lafreniere; LG, Tedeschi, O'Hearn, Barbarossa; C, Levitt, Mandell; RG, Lisiewski, Andruskiewicz; RT, Vasington, Markey; RE, Buchanan, Weiss, Driscoll; QB, Waldron, Butova, Carlson; LHB, Rogalski, Fellows; RHB, Barber, Landone, Stelzman; FB, Avdevich, Atkins, Fields.

Bulkeley	*7*	*20*	*13*	*0–40*

> *Touchdowns—Johnson 3, Rockholz, Crowley, Ealahan. Points after touchdowns—Rockholz 2 (placements); Dorsey 2 (placements). Missed points after touchdowns—Dorsey (placement); Gorra (pass).*

The following week, Bulkeley tied Nashua of New Hampshire, 7–7, in an unofficial New England championship. Bill Kirpiewski scored on a one-yard run in the second quarter for the Tigers.

If the 1941 matchup was a game full of stars for Bulkeley, the 1942 contest highlighted the ones who ride the bench. Specifically, Jim Sullivan.

Sullivan was a substitute end who didn't see much time during the season. But on a rainy November 21 day at the Academy, Sullivan had his greatest day as a high school player.

Bulkeley's Bob Rockholz and NFA's Archie Avdevich had traded touchdowns in the first two quarters of the game, which went to halftime tied at thirteen.

After a scoreless third quarter, the stage was set for Sullivan to enter the game. Wrote the *New London Evening Day*:

> *Sullivan, who has seen little service this season and who served as a pass decoy when he was in action, came into the rightful post of Bulkeley hero No. 1 when he took the touchdown pass on the fourth down and evaded two Norwich tacklers to scamper three steps into the end zone. Sullivan had to make those three steps good as Bulkeley, apparently touchdown bound three plays earlier, was driven back 15 yards via a five-yard penalty and two losses on successive running playas and thus had the goal to go when Rockholz faded to the 30 to throw his game-winning pass…When the final whistle blew Bulkeley fans rushed from the stands to carry Sullivan from the muddy gridiron high on their shoulders.*

The win clinched the Class A championship of the state for Bulkeley, which went 6-1 for the season.

There were no late heroics for the 1943 game, which was played on Thanksgiving. Don Slate and Jack Porter scored two touchdowns, and Bob Davidson and Jim Wetmore also added scores in a 41–6 Bulkeley romp. Bob Nugent scored the lone touchdown for NFA.

Despite the score, the game wasn't without a debate:

> *The game had its controversial angle—a deceptive double shift which pulled the Bulkeley team off-side five times for penalties, three of them giving Norwich first downs. The penalties were confusing to some spectators, inasmuch as the Bulkeley men got back onside before the ball was snapped. However the officials explained that the double shift was legal, since the rules permit repeated shifts within 25 seconds provided there is a definite pause on each shift. Moreover, new rules adopted two years ago provide for a penalty if a player goes offside and makes contact with the opponent, even though he returns on-side before the ball is snapped. The rule is puzzling because some organizations, notably the Rhode Island scholastic conference, does not enforce it, but is governed by the old rule which permitted a player to get back on-side before the ball was snapped, with or without contact.*

If there were any doubts for Bulkeley in 1944, it was how many points it would score and who would try to get in its way because few could stop the Tiger express.

In the opener, Bulkeley beat Hillhouse, a team that went 7-0 in 1943 and earned the Waskowitz Trophy, 24–6. The next week, Bulkeley took care of Stonington, 14–0. Then Amherst (34–6) went down, followed by Hartford (12–6), New Britain (18–6), Windham (51–0), Fitch (38–0) and bitter rival Chapman Tech (7–6).

Enter Norwich Free Academy in the final game of the season on November 18. No matter.

After a scoreless first quarter, Bulkeley ripped off nineteen points in the second quarter. The Tigers added thirteen in the third and twenty in the fourth to win, 52–12, and finish as the only team in the state to go unbeaten and untied. For the second time in four years, the Waskowitz Trophy was theirs.

The *New London Evening Day* reported:

> *Bulkeley used a secret weapon to crush Norwich Saturday. The Bulkeley players appropriately named it H-21. It stood for Bill Hopkins, a*

substitute back, whose jersey number is 21. Hopkins put on what was probably the greatest individual show in the 80-game history of this rivalry. He carried the ball 16 times during the afternoon and compiled the amazing total of 205 yards gained from scrimmage. He scored two touchdowns and threw a 39-yard forward pass for a third.

Besides Hopkins, Bob Daniels scored twice for Bulkeley, and Bob Davidson, Jack Porter, Don Belcher and Bill Kiely all contributed touchdowns.

In coach Bill O'Brien's four years, Bulkeley went 30-2-2 in the greatest four-year span in school history.

The Wildcats, though, stewed. Jimmy Williams, who had taken over as coach in the late 1930s, had a great young team with John Morosky, Frank Vasington and the Tedeschi brothers, George and Bruno. It was time to show their talent.

In 1945, it happened.

Game at a Glance: November 17, 1945

All the pieces came together in 1945, when the Wildcats avenged the four straight losses by beating Bulkeley, 7–2, in front of 4,500 fans at Mercer Field. The win propelled the Associated Press to name undefeated Norwich Free Academy as the state champions.

The 1945 NFA state champions. One year after giving up fifty-two points to Bulkeley, NFA held Bulkeley to two points in a 7–2 win. *Courtesy of Norwich Free Academy.*

The 1945 NFA state champions. The Wildcats won the state championship this year, which, as of 2012, remains the last championship for the school.

As of the writing of this book, it was the last state championship the Wildcats won.

The *New London Evening Day* wrote:

> *Norwich Free academy maintained its hopes for a state football championship by defeating Bulkeley, 7–2, Saturday afternoon at Mercer field in what was definitely the most colorful battle of this three-quarter-century-old gridiron rivalry.*
>
> *The Wildcats' winning score came in the second period with Johnny Morosky, ace Norwich passer, tossing the pigskin to Ray Lukasiewicz in the end zone for a touchdown. Frank Vasington passed to Lukasiewicz for the extra point. Bulkeley's lone score came in the final period when Morosky was tackled in his end zone for a safety.*
>
> *The crowd, officially announced as the largest ever to see a high school football game in this city, will pass the 4,000 mark in paid admissions when all returns are in. Bulkeley spokesmen announced that 3,904 paying customers have already been accounted for and that the ticket sale from downtown stores and some of the local and suburban grammar schools is not yet complete. Add to these complimentary tickets and the legion of gate crashers and fence-vaulting youngsters and the complete attendance probably hit 4,500.*

Air Filled with Passes

Other items which added to the color and excitement of the contest were the 37 forward passes tossed all over the Mercer field. Bulkeley threw 20 and Norwich 17 to set a new game record in this department for eastern Connecticut schools. A combination of five fumbles and five pass interceptions switched the ball from team to team with such suddenness that the huge crowd was in a continuous state of uproar during the entire 48 minutes of fierce play.

If Norwich goes on to defeat Worcester on the academy campus Thanksgiving afternoon, the Wildcats will have a very definite claim to the state title. Weaver, presently leading the scholastic rating sheet, faces a weak Hartford Public team, also on Thanksgiving, and should win easily to wind up undefeated. In some circles the belief is that Weaver did not play a so-called "major opponent" schedule and Norwich might be selected over the unbeaten Green Wave.

Clinch Eastern Conn. Title

At the very worst Norwich can claim the eastern Connecticut schoolboy title on its clean sweep of four area foes. No other eastern Connecticut school has a perfect record in district competition.

Norwich's score came as the result of three forward passes and a pair of running plays in the second period for a 69-yard touchdown march. A long pass from John Morosky to Joe Iacoi netted 44 yards. Morosky lost three yards on an end run but then passed to Red Killeen, who snatched the ball from four Tiger defenders on the Bulkeley six-yard line. Bob Mattio was stopped at the scrimmage line on an attempted buck and Morosky then faded to toss a flat pass to Ray Lukasiewicz, who grabbed the pigskin in the end zone in spite of pass interference on the part of Dick Ballestini, Bulkeley back. Frank Vasington passed to Lukasiewicz on a fake placement for the extra point.

That was Norwich's only chance to score. At no other time did the Wildcats get within 30 yards of the Bulkeley goal as an inspired Bulkeley line played a brilliant defensive game.

BULKELEY THREATENS TWICE

Bulkeley, on the other hand, had two excellent touchdown chances but a penalty halted one drive and the Norwich line arose to stop the other.

Bulkeley's first offensive series of the game opened with Capt. John O'Grady racing 44 yards on a weak sidespin play. That put the ball on the Norwich 30-yard line. The Tigers then marched to the six for a first down from where O'Grady went to the three-yard line only to have Bulkeley penalized for a back in motion. The series ultimately ran out with Bulkeley three yards from the goal.

In the fourth period Bulkeley drove from the Tiger 34 to the Norwich 11 on passes from Jim Carver to Tom Daniels, and Jim Barrett and O'Grady's six-yard line smash. The Tigers again lacked the punch and Norwich took over on downs on the five-yard line. On the first Norwich scrimmage play, Joe Carey, Pete Carchidi and O'Grady swept through the Norwich line to tackle Morosky behind the line for a safety.

Bulkeley had only a little left at this time with the final seconds ticking away and a brief drive that stretched from the Bulkeley 45 to the Norwich 33 came to an abrupt end when Iacoi intercepted a long touchdown pass intended for Daniels. The Bulkeley end had gotten behind the Norwich defender but the pass was short and Iacoi picked it off to preserve the 7–2 margin.

BALLESTRINI INJURED

Bulkeley was sorely handicapped in the second half by the loss of Ballestrini, who suffered a break of his left clavicle (collarbone) midway in the second period. O'Grady, too, suffered a leg injury at the very start of the same period and was unable to drive with his usual force and speed during the remainder of the game. In spite of the injury, O'Grady was still one of the best players on the field.

Al Sitty led the Bulkeley defense, doing an A-1 job in backing up the line. Elsewhere along the forward wall the Tigers charged with their midseason recklessness and spirit.

Morosky's passing, Washington's running and Iacoi's sensational punting headlined the Norwich play. Bingo Johndrow, center, was the Wildcat defensive star.

Statistically, Norwich had the edge in most departments, but most of the ground gained was between the 40-yard stripes. Once the Wildcats moved into Bulkeley territory ten yards or so, they found the going pretty rugged.

Pre-Game Show

The pre-game festivities were the most impressive of any ever put on at any local football game. The Norwich band came on the field first with the fife and drum corps followed by the baton swingers and band. Then the Bulkeley band marched on the field and combining under one leadership, the two bands played the national anthem.

An unusual situation occurred during the closing minutes of the game when the linesmen pulled up the stakes and ran upfield prematurely when it appeared that Norwich had reeled off a first down deep in Bulkeley territory. However, there was an off-side penalty on the play and the ball was called back. There was a delay of a few minutes as the officials tried to relocate the line stakes in their original positions. Some spectators thought that Norwich gained a few yards on the linesmen's mistake.

Lineups:

Bulkeley	Norwich
LE-Daniels	Lukasiewicz
LT-Clemens	T. Lonardelli
LG-Carey	Rathbone
C-Pugsley	Johndrow
RG-Sitty	G. Tedeschi
RT-Carchidi	B. Tedeschi
RE-Barrett	Killeen
QB-Belcher	Iacoi
LHB-Carver	Morosky
RHB-Ballestrini	Madio
FB-O'Grady	Vasington

Bulkeley	0	0	0	2–2
Norwich	0	7	0	0–7

Touchdown—Lukasiewicz.

Point after touchdown—Lukasiewicz (pass from Vasington).

Safety—Morosky (tackled by Carey, Carchidi, O'Grady).

Bulkeley subs—Bosko, Peck, Shumway, Olsen, R. Carver, Burke, Pappadapoulos, Bernstein, Belleisle.
Norwich Subs—Perkins, LaFreniere, T. Haldis, Butova.
Officials—Referee, A.J. McAdam; umpire, F.A. Hopkins; field judge, M.E. Kearns Jr.; linesman, F.P. Austin.
Statistics

	Bulkeley	*Norwich*
First downs	*7*	*10*
Yards rushing	*125*	*132*
Yards passing	*79*	*112*
Passes attempted	*20*	*17*
Passes intercepted by	*2*	*3*
Passes completed	*5*	*7*
Fumbles	*1*	*4*
Own fumbles recovered	*1*	*1*
Punts	*5*	*7*
Average of Punts	*31.6*	*43.8*
Number of penalties	*2*	*6*
Yards penalized	*10*	*60*

More than six thousand fans jammed NFA for the November 16, 1946 game. Bulkeley capitalized on an interception and fumble to pull out a 13–6 win:

The stagnant Norwich Free Academy attack coughed and sputtered often Saturday at the campus and just couldn't get rolling enough to down the tough Bulkeley Tigers. The Acads did manage to get one tally across on a brilliant Johnny Morosky–Joe Iacoi pass but that was virtually the full extent of the NFA attack. The final score was 13–6 in favor of the Bengals and some observers class it as an upset. While their offense was off, the Academy defense was almost rock-ribbed. A record paid attendance of 6,116 saw the game.

The Wildcats drew first blood when they scored early in the first period. An Orange and Black drive had petered out on the Norwich 20 and the Acads took possession of the ball.

The Academy Score
In a drive led by Morosky, the locals picked up a pair of first downs, moving the pigskin up to the Tiger 47. After a couple of running plays had gotten nowhere, Morosky heaved a beautiful aerial to Iacoi, who snagged it and, eluding Safety Man Jim Carver, streaked the rest of the way into pay dirt. This was destined to be the only Red and White score, however, when Ray Lukasiewicz failed to boot the extra point.

The rest of the first period was spent in punt exchanges. The early part of the second quarter saw the 'Cats drive to the Bulkeley 16 at one time but the Tiger forward wall held to thwart the threat. Shortly, Tom Daniels punted the ball to the opposition's 15 to pull the Bengals out of danger. At this point Bulkeley got the break that put them back in the ball game.

Peabody Tallies
Morosky took the ball and faded to throw a pass but he was rushed and forced to get rid of the ball to avoid being thrown for a long loss. He tossed to what he apparently thought was a vacant spot but Bob Peabody, substitute Bulkeley center, popped up in front of it on the 20 and raced, untouched, into the end zone to knot up the score. Bill Walsh failed to kick the extra point and half ended in a 6–6 tie.

Bulkeley in Charge
In the second half the Tigers took complete charge of the struggle. After the Acads had received the kick-off and gotten nowhere on the following few plays, Morosky punted out of bounds on the Orange and Black 44. Bulkeley took to the air via Jim Carver and tossed a pass to Nate Belcher, which brought the ball up to the midfield stripe. When Carver and George Pugsley had picked up a first down on two running plays, Carver fired a long toss to Bill Burke on the Red and White 23 for another first down. The Bulkeley backs alternated in carrying the ball from here on until they had driven to the Norwich 2. On third down with goal to go Burke was thrown for a loss to the 4 by the stiffening NFA forward wall. Carver managed to buck his way off tackle but couldn't quite cross the double stripes and Bulkeley had to give up the ball for

lack of downs. This marked the first of two sensational goal line stands by the home team.

After the Bengals had taken a Wildcat punt on their opponent's 41 and failed to go anywhere on two incomplete forwards, Carver's right arm whipped a pass to Daniels on the seven to again threaten the Academy goal. On two consecutive spins off tackle, Carver and Burke each managed to pick up a yard which placed the ball squarely on the 'Cats five.

Automatic Touchback

Joe Iacoi came to the rescue here when he intercepted a Carver pass in his own end zone to end this Orange and Black threat. The officials ruled this an automatic touchback and the ball was brought out to the 20 of Norwich.

It was apparent, however, that the Academy could not keep stopping the Tiger thrusts short and the inevitable happened in the first minutes of the fourth period. Actually the drive began only two plays after Iacoi's touchdown-interception.

Morosky punted to the Red and White 41. Carver then lugged the ball around the right end on a beautifully executed reverse, running 17 yards to the Academy 24 before he was finally brought down. After an incomplete pass, Carver threw a strike to Belcher on the 17 and Burke carried on two consecutive plays to the 14 for a first down for the victory. The quarter ended here and the game entered its final quarter with neither team ahead.

Over From the Four

Carver changed the situation, however, when, after three plunges had brought the ball to the Norwich four, he spun off tackle on a quick opening play for what proved to be the decisive score. Bulkeley wanted to be sure so Walsh kicked the extra point to put his team ahead 13–6.

Norwich, in desperation, began heaving aerials on nearly every play that they had the ball but the attack clicked only spasmodically and never resulted in a serious threat to the Tiger goal. The Bengals held on to the ball for most of the rest of the time and finally managed to run out the clock.

The victory gives Bulkeley the mythical eastern Connecticut championship.

The fans were entertained during the half time by the all-girl drum and bugle corp of NFA and the Bulkeley band who based their display on a huge anchor arrangement formed to the tune of "Anchor's Aweigh."

This was the season finale for the Tigers, who wound up the year with a record of six wins against two defeats. NFA has one more contest.

Jim Carver, playing his last game in a Bulkeley uniform, turned in one of his best performances of the year, leading the Tigers both offensively and especially in the passing department. George Pugsley also graduates this year and turned in a creditable game, particularly on the defense, as a parting gesture.

Fully 6,500 saw the game, for, in addition to the paid figures, there were the bands, drum corps, etc. Automobiles were parked for over a half mile in all streets adjacent to the campus.

Bulkeley	*Norwich*
Daniels, le	*le, Lukasiewicz*
Neville, lt	*lt, Lonardelli*
Walsh, lg	*lg, Giallombardo*
Stevens, c	*c, Leone*
R. Carver, rg	*rg, Rathbone*
Bosko, rt	*rt, B. Tedeschi*
Peck, re	*re, Killeen*
Belcher, qb	*qb, G. Tedeschi*
J. Carver, lhb	*lhb, Morosky*
Burke, rhb	*rhb, Iacoi*
Pugsley, fb	*fb, Butova*

Bulkeley subs—Shumway, Peabody, Pappadapoulos, Nugovero, Damico, Driscoll, Scacciaferro, Bernstein, Cascio, Olsen.

Norwich subs—Haldis, Leonard, Gatrousis, McNamara, Madio.

Officials—Referee, Hopkins; umpire, Hart; linesman, Higgins; field judge, Austin.

Time of quarters—12 minutes.

Touchdowns: Bulkeley—Peabody; J. Carer. Norwich—Iacoi.

Point after touchdowns: Bulkeley, Walsh (placement). Norwich—None.
Missed points after touchdowns: Bulkeley, Walsh; Norwich—Lukasiewicz.
Statistics:

	Bulkeley	*Norwich*
Yards gained rushing	*180*	*54*
Yards gained passing	*95*	*150*
Passes	*15*	*23*
Passes completed by	*6*	*10*
Passes intercepted by	*1*	*1*
First downs	*11*	*6*
Fumbles	*5*	*6*
Own fumbles recovered	*4*	*4*
Punts	*6*	*6*
Punts average	*38*	*33.2*

Norwich rebounded the next year, pulling out an 18–14 win in front of three thousand fans at Mercer Field when Norwich went on a forty-six-yard drive in the third quarter and scored on Bob Adams's touchdown. John Evans added two scores for Norwich in the first half, while Bulkeley co-captain Bill Burke tallied two touchdowns.

The *New London Evening Day* said, "The annual battle came as something of an anticlimax, following the record-breaking attendance at the Bulkeley-[Chapman] Tech game on Armistice Day, and the usual interest just wasn't there."

GAME AT A GLANCE: NOVEMBER 13, 1948

The year 1948 turned out to be the season to forget for both teams. Norwich entered the final game of the season 1-5, while Bulkeley was 3-4. Still, that didn't deter the rivalry.

When the teams met on November 13, both had ample opportunities to score. But neither one found the end zone in the fourth—and so far, last—scoreless duel between the teams.

The *Norwich Bulletin* reported:

> *The sun broke through a few minutes before the nation's two oldest interscholastic football rivals, Norwich Free Academy and New London Bulkeley, took the field Saturday afternoon at the campus and then proceeded to battle to the fourth and scoreless tie in 73 years of campaigning. This was the 84th meeting of the traditional adversaries.*
>
> *Coach Jimmy Williams' Wildcats closed their season with a record of one victory, five losses and this tie, while Bill O'Brien's Bulkeley team compiled a season's record of three wins, four losses and the tie.*
>
> *NFA threw away its first scoring chance, right in the first period, and, the game ended as time ran out for the Wildcats on Bulkeley's 11-yard line.*
>
> *Norwich kicked off to open the contest and end George Scacciaferro of Bulkeley was tackled on his 35. Bulkeley made little headway and kicked offside on the Norwich 44.*
>
> *The Wildcats then opened a drive, which ended on the Bulkeley nine.*
>
> *Bulkeley then produced a march of its own, with backs Bob Thompson and Bob Eldridge leading the way, which was terminated on the Norwich seven, as a pass, attempted by Bulkeley's Bob McPhail, was blocked.*
>
> *Norwich took over and brought the ball back seven yards before the quarter ended.*
>
> *There was little further doing until Bulkeley produced another scoring threat in this second period, the Tigers being halted within the 20-yard line, but a penalty against the Tigers for having 12 men on the field eased the situation for the Wildcats and the half finally ended with Bulkeley on the Norwich 40.*
>
> *Bulkeley kicked off to open the third quarter and it went to the ten-yard line when Norwich's Shea ran the ball back to his own 49. Quarto gained six, Strickland five, Leist lost four when he fumbled but recovered. Leist and Quarto then produced a first down and Leist again gained, reaching Bulkeley's 18. Strickland missed a Quarto pass that might have meant a touchdown, following which Norwich gave up the ball on downs.*
>
> *The fourth quarter saw Norwich's final threat after the Wildcats took over on Bulkeley's 27 and, featured by a pass, Quarto to Marshall,*

got the ball to the 11, where the contest ended before another play could be run off.

NOTES OF THE GAME

Due to the inclement weather, the crowd was held down to slightly less than the seating capacity. It rained up to a few minutes of starting time. The crowd was estimated at about 2,500.

The NFA drum corps and the band presented colorful exhibitions, "N's" and "B's" being formed during half-time.

No players were seriously injured, although Sistare, Bulkeley player, was taken out with a reported leg injury, which was diagnosed as a sprained ankle.

Most NFA followers came away convinced that the Wildcats had played probably their best game of the season and had produced one of those moral victories, since Bulkeley went into the contest as quite a favorite.

NORWICH

Ends—Izbicki, Tamborra, Marshall, Atterbury.

Tackles—Dobiejko, Archibald, Gernhard.

Guards—Nordoff, Clang.

Centers—DePinto, Bedat.

Backs—Shea, Quarto, Strickland, Leist, Tedeschi, Gadle.

BULKELEY

Ends—Nassetta, Scacciaferro, Welch

Tackles—Shannon, Driscoll, Synoldi, Facas.

Guards—Hill, Manavas, Gigliotti, Manwaring.

Centers—Griffith, Sistare, Stone.

Backs—McPhail, Eldridge, Thompson, Olsen, Hoffner, Burke.

Statistics

	Norwich	*Bulkeley*
First downs	*11*	*11*
Yards gained rushing	*125*	*145*
Passes attempted	*10*	*7*
Yards gained passing	*73*	*53*
Passes completed	*4*	*3*
Punts	*5*	*5*

The 1949 Bulkeley-NFA game, which the Wildcats won 34–14. *Courtesy of the* Norwich Bulletin.

An NFA rally after beating Bulkeley in 1949. *Courtesy of the* Norwich Bulletin.

Average distance of punts	*38*	*34*
Fumbles	*2*	*1*
Own fumbles recovered	*1*	*1*
Penalties	*4*	*2*
Yards lost on penalties	*30*	*10*

On November 19, 1949, Norwich had no problems getting into the end zone on a chilly day at Mercer Field, holding a 15–7 halftime lead en route to a 34–14 win in which the Wildcats outgained the Tigers, 220–75. Sophomore Don Scott scored three times, and teammates Ed Zdancewicz and Johnny Marshall also tallied touchdowns. For Bulkeley, Eugene Brown and Fred Ballestrini reached the end zone.

In a bit of foreshadowing, the *New London Evening Day* reported, "Was this the final Bulkeley-Norwich game in the literal sense? Recent stories as carried by the *Day*, hint at the possibility of a Bulkeley-WMI combine. In 1950, it may be Norwich vs. Bulkeley-WMI High School."

6
TAKING A BREAK
1950–1959

Rumblings had begun in the late 1940s about combining the city's three secondary schools—Bulkeley, Chapman Tech and the Williams Memorial Institute, which was an all-girls' school.

Although it wasn't set in stone, 1950 would be the last time Bulkeley and Norwich Free Academy would meet. On November 18, a crowd of more than three thousand in Norwich saw the home team score a fourth-quarter touchdown to pull out a 13–7 win in which NFA outgained Bulkeley, 264–206. Tom Izbicki and Tom Euell both scored for the Wildcats as NFA won the Eastern Connecticut Conference crown.

Game at a Glance: November 17, 1951

After the 1950–51 school year, the Williams Memorial Institute moved to its present location on the Connecticut College campus and became the Williams School. Bulkeley and Chapman Tech combined to form New London High School. Its new mascot was the Whalers, and its colors were green and gold.

On November 17, 1951, at Morgan Park, the new-look Whalers met the Wildcats in the "inaugural" game. Thanks to a brawl, it would be the final game for two seasons.

Ernie Rokowski and Don Scott were the stars for NFA in 1951.

Opinions still differ today about what happened in terms of who did what. The popular account is that a New London assistant coach slugged NFA senior Don Scott near the end of the game, after Scott took a swing at a New London player following being shoved on the sideline.

It was a rough-and-tumble affair, with the *New London Evening Day* reporting that "several fights between the players were quickly halted by the officials with only one player being banished from the contest."

That didn't faze the Whalers, who pulled out a 22–6 win. Jim Buonocore, who eighteen years later would begin his career as the greatest coach in New London history, was a mite-sized halfback on this team and led the Whalers to victory.

The *Norwich Record*, a sister paper of the *Norwich Bulletin*, wrote:

> *NEW LONDON, Nov. 17—(Special) In one of the biggest upsets of the local football season, an underdog New London Whaler combine completely outplayed a favored Norwich Free Academy 22–6 before a crowd that fell below expectations at Morgan Park today.*
>
> *The victory closed the New London schedule while the Wildcats have yet to meet Brockton at the Massachusetts city on Thanksgiving.*
>
> *To pick out one individual in this victory of the Whalers would perhaps be unfair to the rest of the team but this reporter picks out the brilliant line backing of Arnie Manwaring, pint-sized fullback, who just about steamrolled the Norwich linemen all afternoon.*

Best Since Hopkins

Manwaring's performance of line smashing was one of the best locally since the job Paul Hopkins did against the Wildcats a few years ago for Bulkeley.

The Wildcats, geared to stop the slants and end runs of Jimmy Buonocore and Jimmy Finnegan, were no match for these line blasts which Manwaring completed. He was never stopped and when the Whalers operated from a single wing, a real surprise maneuver for them, Manwaring was unstoppable.

But Manwaring with all his gaining did not score a touchdown, leaving this department to Buonocore, who scored twice, once on a pass, and the other on a handoff from Manwaring, and Finnegan, who ran 38 yards for the first score.

Other Stars

But it would be unfair to say Manwaring was the whole show for the line, with Sal Savona, Larry Marth, John Stadnick, and Phil Lentine keeping the Wildcats at bay most of the game.

For Norwich, Don Scott was never allowed to go too far although he broke away for gains of close to 30 yards several times.

The Whalers showed that they were up for this game of the season when after they failed to gain, Mann kicked to Don Scott on the 35 and the elusive back was nailed back on the 22 trying to find a hole to break through.

The first two plays found the New London line led by Larry Marth, Sal Savona and Phil Lentine shoving Norwich back for a loss of seven yards, causing Scott to try the quick kick weapon, which did not travel too far and New London took over on the Norwich 40.

That was the beginning of the end from here on, except for a brief moment in the second quarter the Wildcats were never a threat.

Lose on Downs

The Whalers, with Manwaring doing the bulk of the carrying, got a first down on the 29 but the Wildcats braced and took the ball away on downs on the 35.

The Wildcats on two plays went to the 40, but on the next play Phil Lentine, line backer, intercepted a short Don Scott pass on the 45 and raced to the 34 before he was brought down.

Two first downs brought the ball to the nine-yard line but after the Wildcats had held for three downs, Don Burke replaced Bobby Murphy in the Whalers lineup and he shot a flat pass to Jimmy Buonocore on the seven and only a fine defensive block by Bob Pirie saved the touchdown, as he did this on the two-yard line.

On the third down, the New London line rushed in with Larry Marth blocking the kick of Pirie and the ball bounced back through the end zone to give the Whalers a safety.

Quarter Ends

The quarter ended with the kickoff but Arnie Mann, who did a fine job of punting all afternoon, booted out of bounds on the Norwich eight-yard line.

It was here that Norwich made its bid for a score as Scott started off the drive by going around left end for 29 yards to the 37. The fine Norwich back again broke loose three plays later with another romp of 29 yards but a clipping penalty pushed the Wildcats back to the 45.

Here Scott passed neatly to Dick Cipriani for a first down on the 20 and the Norwich supporters really perked up.

Wildcats Halted

However on the next play, Scott, on taking a handoff, tripped over his own blocker and lost to the 30-yard line and another five-yard loss to Jerry McCarthy killed the rally.

Two exchanges later, New London took the ball on the N.L. 36 and in four plays moved the 64 yards for the touchdown. Manwaring bulled for a pair of yards; Buonocore on a handoff went off tackle for ten; Finnegan went for three more but Norwich was penalized to the 34 for unnecessary roughness. That possibly made Finnegan mad for the little gamester, who played with a fibre-covered hip pad, went the final 38 yards all by himself on a dash through the middle of a well blocked line. Manwaring added the extra point and the Whalers led 9–0 at half time.

The Whalers showed they had lost none of their spark in the second half as they ripped off two first downs before kicking to Norwich and after the Wildcats could not dent the defensive pattern of the Flannagan team, Pirie kicked to Manwaring on the 27 and he dashed to the Norwich 47 before being brought down.

Single Wing

After clicking off a first down the Whalers then reached down into their bag of tricks and, from a single wing formation, Manwaring started to hit through the line, handing off to Murphy, to pitchout to Finnegan. The Norwich team pulled in to stop the bull thrusts of Manwaring, were dead ducks for a neat pass from Finnegan to Buonocore who caught the 31-yard heave in the end zone all by himself. Manwaring kicked the extra point.

NFA Kickoff Recovered

Norwich was in a daze by this turn of events and were plainly shaken as they allowed the Whalers to recover the kickoff on the 35 as Davis fell on the pigskin. Five plays later, Lou Saunders fumbled on the three-yard line as he could have gone all the way and Ed Fontaine recovered for the Wildcats.

However Norwich elected to gamble on going for a first down the 13 and a fourth-down rush fell way short as Lentine, Savona, and Bigornia all had a hand in the stop.

Two plays later the quarter ended and on the third play of the final quarter Buonocore on a reverse from Manwaring went over for the touchdown.

Almost Get Another T.D.

The Whalers missed another touchdown later in the quarter as Don Burke passed successfully to Bigornia in the end zone but a holding penalty nullified the score.

The Wildcats then marched straight down the field as the passing combination of Carden to Cipriani clicked brilliantly with the hard-running Cipriani jumping high in the end zone out of the clutches of the Whaler defenders to get the touchdown on an 18-yard connection.

OUTBURST NEAR BENCH

Soon after this touchdown the game ended but not before a mild outburst after a play was completed by the New London bench. A few punches were thrown but coaches, officials and the police ended what could have been a sweet riot.

THE STATISTICS

	NL	*NFA*
First downs	*16*	*7*
Yards gained rushing (net)	*228*	*103*
Passes attempted	*10*	*12*
Passes completed	*4*	*4*
Yards gained passing	*74*	*86*
Punts	*3*	*5*
Punting average	*34.3*	*20.4*
Interceptions	*2*	*1*
Fumbles	*2*	*0*
Own fumbles recovered	*2*	*0*
Yards lost by penalties	*70*	*45*

NEW LONDON

Ends—Cochrane, Silva, Bigornia, Callahan, Hutchinson, Tuneski.

Tackles—Savona, D'Amico, Keating, Impelliteri, Gaines

Guards—Nenna, Pudlo, Sullivan, Morth, Stadnick, Duclos, Evanski

Centers—Davis, Lentine, Cooper

Backs—Buonocore, Finnegan, Kelly, Saunders, Manwaring, Brown, Edwards, Burke, Murphy, Mann, Beran, Jetmore, Giordano, Alderson.

NORWICH

Ends—Cipriani, Pirie, Krohn, Reynolds, Osik, Kohanski.

Tackles—Sisco, Gromko, Wisneske, Iacozza, Harb.

Guards—Jennings, Fontaine, Post.

Centers—Lariviere, Murphy.

Backs—Carden, Scott, T. McCarthy, Hewitt, Geissler, R. McCarthy, Baldyga.

Score by periods

Norwich	*0*	*0*	*0*	*6*	*—*	*6*
New London	*2*	*7*	*7*	*6*	*—*	*22*

Scoring: Touchdowns—Finnegan, Buonocore 2; Cipriani. Points after touchdowns—Manwaring 2 (placekicks). Safety—Morth (blocked Pirie's punt, rolled out of end zone).

After a hiatus of two seasons, heads had cooled enough for the rivalry to be renewed. John DeGange, the terrific writer for the *New London Day*, wrote in the November 23, 1954 edition:

> *With or without severance intervals, students can readily become steamed up over a football game like this one. There will be plenty of enthusiasm and rejoicings, and lamentations while the game is being played and after the final result is established. So it promises to be an exciting day, both for those who are merely interested in football and those who focus on the overall spectacle of football game and cheering crowds in an atmosphere charged with traditional rivalry.*
>
> *Besides deciding which school can win the contest, tomorrow's game will be a test of how well the football relations of the two schools have healed during two years of convalescence. The youngsters will be all excited about the game, naturally, but personally we think that if the adults act like adults, everything will be all right.*

A muddy field in Norwich changed the date of the game to November 22, a Monday. Approximately 2,500 watched the Whalers pull out a 27–6 win. Co-captain John Deligeorges scored three touchdowns, and Billy O'Donnell added the other. Co-captain Jimmy Sullivan added three extra points. For Norwich, Walt Korenkiewicz scored in the second quarter.

Coach Harlan M. Sturgis of New London, pleased with the victory, praised the entire New London team and noted that Sullivan "practically killed the Norwich offense before it got started."

A snowstorm that began about two hours before the 2:00 p.m. kickoff of the 1955 game was the story. New London scored fourteen points in the first quarter en route to a 27–6 win. Lou Caldrello scored two touchdowns, and Jimmy Kelly and Charlie Linski added the others. Tom Discordia added three extra points in front of 1,600 at Morgan Park.

The New London team runs off the snowy field after playing NFA in 1955. The Whalers won, 27–0.

The Whalers made it three in a row the following year, scoring a 20–0 win in Norwich. Tom Discordia, Jimmy Kelly and Red Thompson tallied touchdowns, and Jimmy Lusk kicked two extra points.

Game at a Glance: 1957

Like John DeGange, Jack Cruise was a legendary writer at the *New London Day*. He covered sports there for many years, documenting the Whalers' rise in, among other sports, basketball and baseball.

Cruise covered the 1957 game, which was one of the more dramatic contests in the rivalry's history, which by this point had reached ninety-one games. Cruise wrote:

> *New London High School scored a touchdown in the final minutes of play here Saturday afternoon at Veterans Memorial Field to shade traditional rival Norwich Free Academy, 24–20, in a spectacular offensive battle before 3,500 fans.*
>
> *A Hank Carnaroli–Ken Hill pass with about two minutes of play remaining set the stage for the winning score. The pass brought the ball from the Norwich 20 to the one and Carnaroli took it over on the second shot at the line. There was 1:05 of playing time left as Norwich put the ball in play after the kickoff at the 27.*

Hill's Toe Important

New London's touchdown came at a propitious moment. It gave the Wildcats, who had been moving the ball against the Whalers throughout the second half, little time to launch a counterattack. Two plays moved the ball from the Norwich 27 to the 39, but time ran out before a third play could develop.

Although the Carnaroli-Hill pass furnished the climatic punch, the game was decided because the Whalers put the foot back in football. In the final analysis, each team scored three touchdowns, but Hill booted three perfect conversions and then kicked a 27-yard field goal just before the first half ended.

New London's winning drive was set in motion when Hill recovered a Norwich fumble at the Wildcat 45. Four running plays produced a first down at the Norwich 30 and Bob Foley held pretty well in check most of the day by his Wildcats, burst around left end on a double reverse to the 18. A running play lost two yards and two passes were batted down and so it was fourth and 12 to go when Carnaroli faded back and looped a high pass to Hill near the goal. Hill turned just in time to make the catch and fell forward to the one-yard line. Carnaroli scored on the second play.

The Whalers scored on the game's opening play on a bit of brilliant running by Charlie Pinch, who took the kickoff on the five, faked a handoff to Foley, raced to the right and then cut sharply up the field. Joe Birchall shook Pinch in the clear of the 50 with a savage block and the Whalers halfback smartly outmaneuvered the final Norwich defender with a fine change of pace and stiff arm. Hill kicked the goal and New London was in front, 7–0.

Norwich Not Shaken

If the Whalers and their fans thought this sudden burst would crush the Wildcats, they were in for a surprise. Eleven plays later, Norwich had scored on a 58-yard drive with Warner Murphy going over from the two. George Spencer added the extra point on a buck.

Late in the first period, the Whalers roared 67 yards for their second touchdown with Pinch doing most of the ball carrying. He started the drive by sweeping 17 yards from the 33 and had runs of 13, 18, nine and six yards along the way. Pinch went over from the six and hill added the extra point.

The Wildcats didn't take long to get this one back. After Leon Howard had brought the kickoff back to the New London 43, Tony Cosentino faded back and shot a pass to Art Morrissey in the right flat. Morrissey took the ball a step behind the Whaler defender and raced the rest of the way to the goal. This time Spencer was stopped short of the goal on the try for point.

With time running out in the second period, Pinch broke loose for runs of 20 and 19 yards to get the Whalers down to the Norwich 17. On fourth down, hill kicked a 27-yard field goal from a difficult angle and the Whalers led 17–13 at halftime.

Norwich took the second-half kickoff back to the 28 and moved from there for a touchdown in ten plays. Sweeps by Howard and Murphy were the big gainers in this drive, but the key play was a fourth-down screen from Cosentino to Howard that brought 26 yards and a first down at the New London four. Spencer bolted into the end zone on third down and Morrissey kicked the extra point.

That was all the scoring until the final playoff, but each team had threats. The Wildcats advanced to the New London 12 in the third period and the Whalers' Warren Whitehouse bolted 29 yards to the Norwich eight before fumbling at the start of the fourth period.

Statistics About Even

The statistics show how even the struggle was. Norwich had 16 first downs to 15 for the Whalers and 284 rushing to 248 for the Whalers. Norwich added 117 yards through the air lanes, while the Whalers had only 31, but they had the big play at the finish.

Pinch had a tremendous afternoon and was clearly the best back on the field. He carried the ball 21 times for 165 yards, an average of almost eight yards per try. Add to this his 95-yard kickoff run and you can see he covered plenty of important ground.

Hill was another outstanding player for the Whalers. Besides providing six points with his toe and catching the big pass, Hill recovered the fumble that opened the drive.

The Whalers by winning kept alive their record of never having lost to Norwich in the five games played between the schools.

New London closes out its season Thanksgiving Day when it takes on Robert Fitch at 10 a.m. at Veterans Memorial Field.

Norwich

Ends—Fitch, Macarchuk, Blinderman, Piechowski.

Tackles—DeBartolo, Kreger, Olsiewski, Chey, Cipriano.

Guards—Sangermano, Scheiber, Tedesco, Ramsden, Renshaw.

Centers—Holt, Freeman, Kudej.

Backs—Cosentino, Murphy, Butler, Spencer, Orsluk, Paparelli, Bouleware, Howard, Lebejko, Molkenthin, Morrissey, Dunion.

New London

Ends—Hill, Epps, Braun, Messina, Sanjuan.

Tackles—Fischer, Birchall.

Guards—Carver, Lake, Mark.

Centers—Woodworth, Saunders.

Backs—Carnaroli, Pinch, Foley, Whitehouse, Butchka, Kuvakanka, Raymond, Silvestri, Thompson, Stummer.

Score by quarters:

New London	*7*	*10*	*0*	*7*	—	*24*
Norwich	*7*	*6*	*7*	*0*	—	*20*

New London scoring: Touchdowns, Pinch 2, Carnaroli. Conversions, Hill 3 (placements). Field goal, Hill (27 yards).

Norwich scoring: Touchdowns, Murphy, Morrissey, Spencer. Conversions, Spencer (rush); Morrissey (placement).

Norwich Free Academy finally broke through against New London on November 22, 1958, winning 8–6 in Norwich. The *Day* reported:

Breaks were the deciding factors in Saturday morning's 8–6 victory for Norwich Free Academy over New London High at Norwich.

Both touchdowns of the game were aided by breaks as was the safety which gave Norwich's Wildcats their final two-point margin of victory.

New London got a break in the first period, when it recovered a partly blocked Norwich punt on the Norwich 33 and went on from there to its lone touchdown.

The 1958 NFA team snapped a four-game losing streak in 1958 with an 8–6 win.

Norwich, on its drive to tie the score, got a couple of breaks.

The first was a 15-yard roughing penalty against New London which moved the ball into Whaler territory.

The second came moments later when Norwich, faced with a fourth down and eight yards to go situation, elected to try for it via a pass. The aerial thrown by quarterback Bill Molkenthin, sailed almost into the arms of a New London defender but, somehow or other, it bounced out of his hands and over his head into the waiting arms of astonished halfback Frank Paparelli of Norwich who carried to the 16 before being brought down. Norwich went on from there for its touchdown to tie the count.

Still another break played a big role in the outcome.

PUNT SETS UP SAFETY

With only seconds remaining until the half, Norwich elected to punt from its own 38 on fourth down and six yards to go. The kick, by Jon Scheiber, sailed high into the air and landed on the New London 22. It took a wild bounce, high into the air and down again.

The second time it landed, it bounced crazily toward the New London goal with NLHS safetyman Mike Gerity in pursuit.

Gerity caught up with the ball on about the two-yard line and quickly picked it up. However, his momentum carried him the remaining distance over the goal line and Norwich end Nick Macarchuk, who got downfield fast, hit Gerity before the Whaler back was able to move out of the end zone for a two-point safety.

The wild bounce, Gerity's being carried into the end zone by his momentum and Macarchuk's quickness in getting downfield and dropping Gerity with a perfect hit all added up to victory for Norwich.

Coach Larry Bouley of Norwich was "pleased with the showing of the entire team."

Carrying the offensive burden for the Wildcats and "doing a good job of it" were Scheiber and Leon Howard, both of whom picked up hunks of yardage time and again in running from the single wing.

Bouley was particularly pleased over the result in that it marked Norwich's first win over new London in the new series which began with the 1951 merger of Chapman Tech and Bulkeley School into a single city-owned-and-operated New London High.

Harlan M. Sturgis, NLHS coach, thought New London did "a good job defensively," but was quick to add "we were lacking when it came to offense."

Sturgis agreed the "deflected pass" in Norwich's touchdown drive was "as important a play as there was in the game."

Now New London High has three days—today through Wednesday—to prepare for Thursday morning's Thanksgiving Day clash with across-the-river rival Robert E. Fitch High, a game set for a 10 a.m. start at Veterans Memorial Field.

In the final game of the decade, New London beat Norwich, 14–6, on November 21 at the academy. Chuck Ashburn scored on a forty-six-yard run, and Fred Fabricant added a fifty-five-yard touchdown. Fred Butler hauled in a Billy Discordia pass for the two-point conversion. For Norwich, Sheridan Farrah scored in the second quarter.

7
A MILESTONE AND THE GAME
1960–1969

By 1960, high school football was taking a cue from the professional game. Better protection—facemasks, for example—was becoming the norm, and players weren't going two ways. There were more specialized players who took on specific roles for their teams, allowing rosters to fill up at both schools.

New London and Norwich Free Academy began to see an uptick in the number of students, thanks to baby boomers. NFA, for example, was well over two thousand students at this point. Still, in the first rivalry game of the 1960s, it was New London who held the upper hand, winning 32–0 to finish its season 7-2.

Everything changed in 1961 for the Wildcats.

The team went 7-1-1 and had clinched the Capitol District Conference Championship the week prior to meeting New London on November 17. The Whalers didn't stand a chance. NFA rolled up twenty-eight points in the first half and cruised to a 42–8 win, the biggest triumph for the Wildcats since a 39–0 victory in 1907. Paul Morosky scored two touchdowns, including one on a seventy-yard run, and passed to Ken Vendola for a forty-nine-yard score. Johnny Leone also had two touchdowns, and Bob Alves returned an interception fifty-seven yards for a score.

The Whalers' offense couldn't get going at all; in fact, their lone touchdown came on Billy Butchka's ninety-two-yard kickoff return.

Right: The 1960 New London–NFA game. New London shut out NFA for the third time in seven years in 1960.

Below: The 1960 New London team shut out NFA 27–0.

Norwich kept the good times rolling into the 1962 game. On November 12, a Monday, New London held a 22–12 lead heading into the final quarter on touchdowns from Dave Williams (eight-yard pass from Dave Connors), Bill Foye (four-yard pass from Connors) and Connors's one-yard run. However, NFA saved the best for last. Wrote Bob Nauta of the *New London Evening Day*:

> *But the Norwich Wildcats fought back, closed the gap to four points via a 72-yard scoring march midway through the final stanza and then won*

This page: The 1963 New London–NFA game. NFA beat New London, 22–14, in 1963 for the Wildcats' third win in a row.

the game when fullback Art Lacy bulled over from the one-yard stripe on the final play of the game.

That's right, the final play of the game.

Time ran out as Lacy took a handoff from quarterback John Borst and smashed into the center of the line and over for the touchdown which settled the issue in another chapter of the nation's oldest schoolboy football rivalry.

Starting in 1963, the rivalry took place in the beginning of the season for a few years. The time of month didn't matter. NFA won its third game in a row in the rivalry thanks to two touchdowns from Bob Dunn in a 22–14 win on its home field. John Padgett also scored for the Wildcats, while Mel Williams picked up a Padgett fumble and rumbled ninety yards for one of New London's scores.

Paul Foye, one of a number of great Foyes to walk through New London's halls, snapped the streak on September 19, 1964, with a performance for the ages. After NFA took a 6–0 first-quarter lead on John Padgett's fifty-two-yard run, Foye played a game of "anything you can do, I can do better" by recording a sixty-five-yard touchdown run to tie the game.

The score stayed tied at six until the third quarter, when Foye received a punt at his thirty-one-yard line and ran all the way for a score to put the Whalers ahead, 12–6. And the score stayed that way.

For the ninety-ninth game, the rivalry moved back to its rightful place near the end of the season. New London sophomore guard Bob Long picked up a fumble and ran twenty-eight yards for a touchdown to break

The 1964 New London–NFA game. New London came back with a 12–6 win in 1964.

The 1965 New London–NFA game. The Whalers won the 1965 game, 13–0.

NFA coach Larry Bouley in 1965.

a scoreless halftime stalemate. The Whalers added some insurance later in the quarter when John Ellis, one of New London's all-time athletic heroes, scored on a seven-yard run and added the extra point for the eventual 13–0 victory.

Ellis also was a standout baseball player, for which he became well known. He spent thirteen seasons as a catcher/first baseman in the Major Leagues, getting called up to the New York Yankees in 1969. He also played for the Cleveland Indians and Texas Rangers before retiring in 1981. In fact, he was the Indians' first designated hitter in 1973 and, the following year, caught Dick Bosman's no-hitter. He finished with a .262 average and sixty-nine home runs.

Game at a Glance: November 11, 1966

Not surprisingly, the 100th game provided plenty of fanfare in eastern Connecticut. One week before the game, a large banquet was held on the Norwich Free Academy campus to celebrate the upcoming game. Jack Cruise of the *New London Day* covered the November 7 ceremony:

> *The anniversary week noting the 100th football game between New London and Norwich got off to a roaring start last night as 500 persons jammed their way into the Norwich Free Academy cafeteria for a chicken dinner.*
>
> *It was a night of reminiscing and remembrances and everybody enjoyed the program, which moved swiftly under the guiding hand of Toastmaster Art McGinley, sports editor of the* Hartford Times.
>
> *The guest speaker, Sam DeLuca of the New York Jets, failed to appear, but the only one who seemed to mind was the man who played a major part in arranging the affair—Howard Dickenman, the NFA director of athletics.*
>
> *Dickenman said he had written DeLuca and given him instructions on how to get to the academy. "I closed the letter by saying I had thrown the blocks and it was up to him to get through. I guess he took the wrong holes."*
>
> *Dickenman said he had called the DeLuca home earlier in the evening and had been told the Jets player had left. Dickenman said he was upset because the player had "failed this group of youngsters."*
>
> *But the program continued as Jim Williams, a former NFA player and head coach and an assistant to Head Coach Larry Bouley, showed film clips of former Norwich–New London action.*

The 1966 New London–NFA game, the 100th game of the rivalry.

The program took about three and a half hours and yet moved quickly. The youngsters ate well and seemed to enjoy the stories told by the elder statesmen of the series.

Veteran of the speakers was Coroner Edward G. McKay, who both played and coached at NFA from 1910 through 1922 with time off for service in World War I.

McKay told of early problems, such as one timer who let the game continue until Norwich went ahead, then called a halt to the contest.

Then, he said, there was the time the school had a game with Windham and only ten players. "We went down to the drug store—

where people hung around in those days—and found Joe Cano. He not only played, but fell on a loose football for the winning touchdown."

McKay said he was looking over the large football squads of the two schools and noted "we used to have to play one side of the line against the other." McKay also told about the old equipment and how "we used to take some felt, put a hole in it and make shoulder pads."

McKay, in a closing message to the boys, said, "You can't all be stars, but you should stay with the squad and not drop out."

With Judge S. Victor Prince unable to attend, Pericles (Pat) Haleftiras, a quarterback for four Bulkeley teams from 1928 through 1931, was New London's first speaker. He told of the first two games he played in against Norwich and said "we won moral victories and were told we played very well."

"Then," he added, "we went across the river and got this little fellow (William F. O'Brien) and things changed." Haleftiras and the Tigers of 1931 were unbeaten, untied and unscored upon in Eastern Connecticut Conference play and beat Norwich, 28–0.

Swings and Swipes

At this point, Haleftiras, a former O'Brien assistant and at one time head coach at Admiral Billard Academy, took a few swings at modern football. "The boys of today are definitely bigger, definitely faster and better equipped, but they don't have the command of fundamentals the older ones had."

In an obvious swipe at the modern era of the coach calling the plays, Haleftiras said, "A team is only as strong as its quarterback. It's an injustice to the boys to have someone else calling the plays. The youngsters out there know better who they can handle."

Perhaps one of the reasons DeLuca was not missed was because a former National Football League star—Gil Bouley—was there. The older brother of the present NFA head coach was a star lineman for the Wildcats in the late '30s and then moved on to All-America honors with Boston College and a pro career with first the Cleveland Rams and then the LA Rams.

Bouley introduced young men who had made their marks in college and the world, including Raymond (Pop) Congdon, a former teammate at NFA. Bouley called Congdon "a great punter and tackle." He also asked Charlie Weiss, who starred at fullback for the Wildcats and Cornell, to take a bow and noted, "Charlie happens to be the uncle of New London Coach Bob."

Bouley also thanked Marty Gilman, football equipment manufacturer, "for his influence in an early phase of my life." He mentioned how Gilman, back in 1938 when Frank Leagy was an assistant at Fordham lecturing at a sports clinic, told him "this fellow will be one of the coaching greats some day." Then in an aside to Gilman, Bouley said, "You're a real prophet, Marty."

Bouley urged the boys to "start being leaders on the campus. It's the thing to do, it will make your parents happy and it will make for successful teams."

SWEAT AND SPIRIT

Dr. Joseph Murray, a great competitor as a little man in sports at Bulkeley School in the '40s, told of spirit being the big factor in the success of the 1941 state championship Bulkeley School team. "We had lost to Norwich the year before and had lost for several seasons, but the spirit began building up in the summer when we started conditioning early."

Murray said, "The sweating in August paid off for us and kept us in good shape all year." He said, "The spirit stayed with us all year, too."

Murray introduced Bob Rockholz, the team's halfback. "Bob was our punter, passer and did just about everything. He was a unanimous choice for all-state, too," he concluded.

Tom Izbicki, the final Norwich speaker, limited most of his remarks to humorous anecdotes of the academy days when he was a student and introduced several contemporaries. At the conclusion, he pleaded "for a nice game Friday, a good job by all the boys and a six-point winning edge for Norwich."

NLHS Principal William L. Foye said he was happy to have a part in the 100th anniversary and "hoped somebody is doing the same thing 100 years from now—planning a time such as this." He said the series had had its ups and downs, but the sportsmanship had been good.

Principal Paul Petrich of NFA said he was the fifth principal as the school's administrator, dating back to 1875. He said most of the Norwich games in the series "were played about 100 yards from this room on the campus." He said one early game was played at Chelsea Park and a couple "in an open pasture at East Great Plains." He said the relationship between the cities "had been great" and promised more of this in Friday's game. Turning to Foye, he said, "I hope you become gracious losers."

Sadness and Happiness

William F. O'Brien, director of athletics for New London High and a former Bulkeley School coach, said he came to "this field about this time 42 years ago and I've been doing the same ever since. Some days I've left here sad and other days I've left here happy, but always felt in coming up here we were going to have a good game."

O'Brien said the series had been one where a school would win three or four years in a row and the other would reciprocate. He said he felt in Friday's game both teams would give their all and told his players "you will remember this game for years."

New London's Coach Bob Weiss said he had been to his first football game as a boy at the academy and added, "I hope Friday isn't my last." He said his new coaching staff had really inherited something in this 100th game, but added, "We're good losers." The game, he said, "should be a good one, but NFA is favored because of its record."

Larry Bouley said he felt "as if I've been at the academy all my life." He said he appreciated the "freedom of movement where I can do the things which I feel are right without being criticized." He praised his coaching staff as being loyal in good and bad times "and putting up with me."

Bouley said the Wildcats had been in a "giving mood of late, but this is going to cease. After what I saw this afternoon on the practice field, anybody that gets anything out of us will have to take it."

Trophy Is Prize

Mayor Harvey N. Mallove of New London was unable to attend because of a council meeting, but sent along his greetings. In a letter to

Principal Foye, Mallove wrote: "In a country as young as our America, 100th anniversaries are indeed very rare and you, as the principal of one of the two participating schools, must be proud of the part you and your student body are playing in this 100th meeting."

Mallove, who asked Foye to represent the city at the affair, further wrote, "We will be sure to properly recognize this significant event in the records of our meeting of tonight so that we can be sure this will properly be recorded in New London's written history."

Solon B. Silverstein of New London, representing the New London County Touchdown Club, presented plaques to both Foye and Petrich as permanent record places for future scores of the series.

Displayed at the head table was the huge trophy to be presented to the winner of Friday's game. It was given by the Chambers of Commerce in the two cities. Dickenman quipped to the gathering, "In the event of a tie, duplicate prizes will be given."

Coaches Weiss and Bouley presented Revere bowls to "workhouses of their squads." Receiving the bowls were:

NORWICH

Walter Anuszewicz, Michael Arpin, William Bellisle, Thomas Bielecki, Robert Brown, Robert Butrymowicz, David Casey, Michael Debartolo, Randall Dietering, Stanley Dmuchowski, George Gianacopoulos, Peter Galligan, Brian Glenney, Victor Hadam, Darryl Horelik, Paul Jakubielski, Peter Keegan, Charles Levanto, Ralph Liepold, Russell Lucy, George Minzy, Michael Morosky, Thomas Moretti, Joseph Oaks, James Pepin, Robert Przekop, Joseph Quarto, Robert Roche, Edward Ryan, Joseph Scholaro, Terry Sinay, Paul Thornton, Steve Urban, Robert Valentine.

Coaches, Laurent H. Bouley, James Buonocore, James Giordano, Rene Ledoux, James Williams.

Principal Paul Petrich, Trainer John Tedeschi and Director of Athletics Howard B. Dickenman.

NEW LONDON

Gregory Apanashk, Glenn Bernoudy, Keven Booth, John Brennan, Joseph Brennan, Kenneth Bryant, Robert Burnham, Philip Call, Anthony Christopher, Robert Cramer, Ernest Douglas, Vita Fatone, Louis Fiano,

George Gierhart, James Grady, Paul Hann, Anthony Harrison, John Hodge, James Jones, Marvin Key, Roderick Lake, Martin Leff, Robert Long, Juan Madry, Dennis Maggi, Samuel Manuel, Howart Martell, Richard McNamara, Dana MacNamee, Robert Perry, Steven Reagan, Jeffrey Schneider, Monty Speedwell, Reginald Sutton, Kirk Talley.
Coaches Robert Weiss, Robert Brigockas, Richard Conover, Louis Rovero, William Lessig.
Mayor Harvey N. Mallove, Medeiros, Principal William L. Foye, Director of Athletics, William F. O'Brien, and Faculty Manager, George H. Gregory.

More than five thousand people filled Norwich Free Academy's stands to see the game that was held on a Friday (November 11), but it was the visiting team that came away with the prize. Jack Cruise wrote:

New London High School's football team saved its finest hour for its biggest crowd of the season yesterday as the fired-up Whalers romped over favored Norwich Free Academy, 28–12, before 5,220 paying fans at the academy campus.

Taking command at the very outset and never allowing the Wildcats to get their attack going with any consistency, the Whalers hit their high total of the season in recording victory in this contest billed as the 100th in the nation's oldest scholastic gridiron rivalry dating back to 1875.

On their way to victory, the Whalers even overcame a couple of tough breaks which might easily have upset a team for which the breaks have

New London's Juan Madry sprints right for a long gain as Bob Long blocks in the 1966 game.

not been going right all year. But it was obvious the Whalers came to win—and nothing else.

At the outset, New London held the Wildcats and forced a poor punt which traveled only to the Norwich 37, but a Whaler secondary man foolishly touched the ball while it was rolling and Norwich recovered.

FUMBLES AT FIVE

Given a shot in the arm, Norwich marched to the New London 22 before the Whalers stiffened and took the ball on downs. Then Juan Madry raced 64 yards on a simple cutback in which the line blocking was simply devastating, but fumbled when hit at the Norwich five and the Wildcats recovered.

Once again, however, the Whalers forced a poor punt and this time got the ball at the Norwich 28. They scored in six plays from there, John Brennan going over from the one on the first play of the second quarter and Bob Long rushing for the two extra points.

Norwich blocked a punt at the New London three to force a scoring opportunity early in the second period, but the Whalers held and took the ball at the two. But when New London kicked out to its 37, Norwich scored in two quick thrusts, one a 32-yard pass play from Paul Jakubielski to Bob Brown. Joe Scolaro took it over from the five, but Jakubielski was thrown short of the goal in a try for two points.

Norwich, trying to move ahead in the closing minutes of the half, had an aerial backfire as George Gierhart picked the ball out of the air at the Norwich 45 and sped down the sidelines for six points.

FIELD GOAL TRY ALMOST COSTLY

Before the half ended, Jim Jones had intercepted a Norwich pass and set up a field goal try by Bob Cramer from the NFA 25. The kick was short and almost cost the Whalers as Mike DeBartolo, a good two-way threat for the Wildcats all day, caught the ball at the goal and returned it to midfield. He had only one New London man and a swarm of blockers in front of him when he was knocked outside at midfield.

The Whalers moved 43 yards in seven plays for their third score midway through the third quarter. Ernie Douglas got the touchdown on a ten-yard pass from Brennan into the flat and Cramer kicked the goal to make it 24–6.

Norwich struck back for a score in the fourth quarter, going 55 yards in five plays as the Wildcats switched from the T to the single wingback. Pete Keegan went the last 15 on a power play over his own right tackle, but the try for two points failed and that hurt the Wildcats, For with about ten minutes left, they still needed two touchdowns to triumph. They didn't get one.

With Norwich gambling on a fourth-and-12 situation in the final five minutes at midfield, the Whalers got the ball at the Norwich 46 and drove for another touchdown in 12 plays. Douglas scored from the three as Brennan directed the attack smartly, throwing one key pass to Madry to keep the drive going.

Play Fitch Thanksgiving Day

Norwich filled the air with passes in the final minute and a half, but connected twice and got only as far as the New London 43.

The Whalers will now be idle until Thanksgiving Day when they play Fitch in the traditional clash. Norwich concluded its season with yesterday's game and wound up with two triumphs against seven losses.

In a halftime ceremony, footballs used in the first and second periods were presented to Principals William L. Foye and Paul Petrich of New London and Norwich respectively. The ball in the second half will go to the Football Hall of Fame in New Brunswick, N.J., with the score inscribed.

New London

Ends—Cramer, Hodge, Bryant, Burnham, Kosztiala.

Tackles—Regan, Hann, Brennan.

Guards—McNamara, Fiano, Maggi.

Centers—Perry, Leff.

Backs—Brennan, Jones, Madry, Long, Fatone, Douglas, Call, Gierhart.

Norwich Free Academy

Ends—Brown, Horelik, Morrison, Thornton.

Tackles—Arpin, Butremovich, Casey, Levanto, Moretti, Valentin, Verville.

Guards—Dmuchowski, Liepold, Lucy.

The 1967 New London team won its fourth in a row in the series, 37–21.

Backs—DeBartolo, Glenney, Jakubielski, Keegan, Pepin, Roche, Scolaro.

New London	*0*	*14*	*7*	*7–28*
Norwich	*0*	*6*	*6*	*0–12*

NL—Brennan, 1 run (Long rush)
N—Scolaro, 5 run (rush failed)
NL—Gierhart, 45 run (rush failed)
NL—Douglas, 10 pass from Brenann (Cramer kick)
N—Keegan, 15 run (rush failed)
NL—Douglas, 3 run (Cramer kick)

New London didn't give up in the 1967 game either, scoring twenty-nine second-half points to pull out a 37–21 victory. The Whalers racked up 428 total yards, including 264 on the ground. Juan Madry scored twice, and John Brennan threw two touchdowns, including one to Jim Gittens that covered 67 yards.

GAME AT A GLANCE: NOVEMBER 16, 1968

It all set the stage for the 1968 game, which was the defining moment in this rivalry. The game is still mentioned today as one of the best games between the two cities in any sport.

The 1968 NFA coaching staff, *from left to right*: assistant coach Jim Buonocore, assistant coach James Williams, head coach Jim Giordano and assistant coach Merrill Thoresen.

The 1968 team won the seminal game in the series, 37–33.

Exactly one week prior to Harvard's 29–29 "win" over Yale in "The Game," New London and Norwich Free Academy squared up in the 102nd meeting. In 1993, Jim Konrad of the *Norwich Bulletin* wrote a retrospective of the game:

> *There are some questions that need to be answered.*
>
> *The first ones are tough.*
>
> *Did Ward Eccles have possession of that last-minute pass from Paul Jakubielski in the end zone long enough for it to be a touchdown—which*

would have given Norwich Free Academy a miraculous come-from-behind victory over top-ranked and undefeated New London?

Or did defender Tim Lewis clearly have control of the ball?

Both players went up for the ball, and—for an instant—both came down with it. But Lewis came away with it, the official ruled interception and New London escaped with a 37–33 victory.

Twenty-five years later, the ruling is a foregone conclusion for the people of New London.

"There's only one guy whose opinion counts," Whalers center Rich Foye said.

For those in Norwich, it is still a hot topic, one they'll argue as long as you let them.

Here's another question:

Was the 1968 NFA–New London game, the 102nd version of the nation's oldest high school football rivalry, the best football game ever played in Eastern Connecticut?

You can't find an argument for that. And if you have one, you better be packing some ammunition. Because those who played and coached, and the thousands who circled NFA's football field, remember Nov. 16, 1968, a cold, miserable Saturday, as if it were yesterday.

They remember NFA scoring 27 straight points and coming back three times, they remember John Brennan throwing five touchdown passes for New London, and they remember the final touchdown that almost was.

And their feelings about the game haven't mellowed with age.

"For those too young and missed it, it's sad," said Jim O'Neill, then a young New London booster and now the school's athletic director. "I get goose bumps just thinking about it. It was a once-in-a-lifetime event."

Any season, the NFA–New London rivalry was the big game of the year. But in 1968, you got the feeling The Game could become something special.

NFA, led by Jakubielski, was having its best season in five years at 7-2. The Wildcats were averaging 30 points a game.

New London, meanwhile, was marching with ease toward the Capitol District Conference title. Calling itself the Green Machine, it was a squad that averaged *51 points a game and gave up only nine, rolling over opponent after opponent. The Whalers' closest game was a 38–12 victory over East Hartford the week before.*

"Waterford, St. Bernard, we kind of blew them away," New London guard Ron Maggi said. "They were just another team. Norwich had to be reckoned with, just because of the rivalry. Anything can happen."

With so much riding on this game, especially for New London, it was hard for the local newspapers to print too much about it.

But they tried.

"Without question, we overhyped it," said Tim Tolokan, who covered NFA for the Bulletin. *"It was just a high school game but if you look back on it…that game was made to be all-world."*

Each school had its own newspaper: NFA had the Bulletin *and New London had the* Day.

The week of The Game, both had features on different facets of the game—the coaches, the quarterbacks, the offenses, the defenses. There were statistics, weather reports, analyses, loads of photos and point spreads; the Whalers were consensus three-touchdown favorites.

Even with the glut, the hype was rarely repetitious and usually stimulating. Comparisons were made between the quarterbacks, Jakubielski for NFA and New London's Brennan—and they were very comparable. Each had thrown for 16 touchdowns and both were good runners and kickers.

New London coach Bob Weiss was always good for a quote. He said, in a variety of ways, that New London was definitely the better team and should win.

The coverage bordered on the ridiculous, but the public couldn't get enough. And pity the seven other games on the schedule that weekend. One report even went so far to say The Game was "the only one with any sort of real values riding on it."

"If you lived in eastern Connecticut, this thing was in your face every day," said Tolokan, now an associate athletic director at UConn. "Even if you had other coverage, you had to squeeze it to make sure you didn't squeeze (New London–NFA) coverage."

The public wasn't just observing the weeklong festivities. It was an active and enthusiastic participant. Players were offered luck and encouragement on the street by people they didn't know, and banners went up in each town. One Norwich store off I-395—at the exit the Whalers' team bus would take to get to NFA—had a monstrous "Beat New London" sign across its front.

New London, meanwhile, was getting into the act. O'Neill, the young officer in the fledgling booster club, helped sell gold Whaler hats. "The crowd was filled with them," he said. "I think we sold 1,000 hats that week."

"It was more of a rivalry between two towns," New London lineman Joe Brennan said. "That's what got the people involved."

And the crowd?

The official gate was 4,400, a number far short of the actual attendance.

Before NFA's Alumni Hall was built, stands were on both sides of the field. Add the sea of fans who were up against the ropes circling the field, the ones on the rocks and hill on the opposite side of the school and the brave or foolish sitting in the trees, and the total ballooned to an estimated raucous 6,000.

"Once you hear the roar of the crowd, you never forget it," said John Tedeschi, NFA's trainer and jack-of-all-trades. "But that crowd was exceptional."

After about 27 minutes, it looked as if the local sportswriters were pretty good prognosticators and Dan Ruffo had a good reason to throw up.

Ruffo, NFA's burly senior fullback, would get so worked up thinking about upcoming games he would get physically ill and miss Thursday practices.

"Some of the guys who didn't know about it would run over and yell, 'Mr. Tedeschi, Mr. Tedeschi, Danny's barfing.'" Tedeschi said.

"I said, 'That's good, he's thinking about the game.'"

The Wildcats as a team were looking a little sick.

After an early field goal by Jakubielski—only the second time all season New London had trailed—Brennan and the Green Machine went to work.

NFA coach Jim Giordano's plan was to stop the Whalers' vaunted running game and make New London win through the air. The Whalers had Juan Madry and Monte Speedwell at halfback. Albie Eccleston, a starting defensive back, was moved to fullback because Tony Harrison had suffered a season-ending neck sprain against East Hartford the week before.

The first half of Giordano's plan worked well. The Wildcats' front line was stingy, and was helped by the week of rain and occasional snow that muddied the field. New London had only 79 rushing yards in the game.

Stopping the pass was another story.

In the first half, Brennan threw touchdown passes to Speedwell (17 yards) and Kevin Booth (52 yards), and Madry plunged in from the 1.

Jakubielski, meanwhile, struggled, throwing four interceptions in the half, three by Ed Ritter. The result was an 18–3 New London lead at halftime.

"Once they got the ball rolling, we fell back in awe against those guys," said Eccles, a split end for NFA. "They were good, they had all the tools.

"But at halftime we said we had all the tools, too. Let's go out and do something."

The Wildcats not only were losing to the Whalers, but to the tension of the big game: Cramps were taking a toll. Cramps usually affect athletes on hot and muggy days, when dehydration becomes a factor. But the weather that day was cold and overcast.

"Dr. (Christopher) Glenney said it was just the anxiety, that we were too tense, that we had to calm down," Eccles said. "We weren't going to calm down in a game like this."

They were getting beat up. Tom Bielecki, NFA's center and linebacker, remembers getting hit in the head near the end of the half—he thinks it was by Brennan's thigh trying to tackle the quarterback. He passed out during halftime but went back in and played the second half.

"I wanted to play," Bielecki said. "We wanted to beat them. That's what it was all about."

But it didn't appear things would get better when the second half started.

On the first play from scrimmage, New London linebacker Reggie Sutton pounced on an NFA fumble at the Wildcats' 27. Four plays later, Brennan hit Reggie Wheeler for a 15-yard touchdown and the Whalers led 25–3.

It might have been a good time for a patented Clyde Parker head slap.

Parker, NFA's senior tackle and linebacker, was regarded as the meanest and toughest player on the team.

"Clyde was the guy who would wait out in front of his house to beat up the paper boy," Tedeschi said. "And if he got away, Clyde was (mad) the whole day."

Although Eccles called him "a maniac," Parker was a perfectionist. If he opened a hole, he expected his teammates to use it.

"Everybody knew what they were supposed to do," said Parker, who says he has calmed down since high school. "Some guys needed a slap in the head…Those guys knew what they had to do and how to play the game."

There wasn't any slapping going on—because at that moment, the game suddenly changed.

Nobody can agree why. Maybe the Whalers, despite Weiss' urging to avoid overconfidence, thought that touchdown put the game away. Maybe the Wildcats, in their final game, had too much pride to watch their hated rivals walk all over them at home.

"We were killing them at halftime, we thought it was a big joke," said Tom Major, a sophomore linebacker for New London. "Coach Weiss told us they weren't going to give up but we were pretty cocky… Let's face it, it was a letdown and they came back."

Almost with a vengeance.

It was started by a little junior halfback named Leo Bawza. Jim Buonocore, an NFA assistant coach, had coached Bawza in freshman baseball. Before the start of the '68 football season, he went to the Bawza home in Lisbon and recruited Leo to play football.

The first day of practice, Bawza got one of the last helmets, and it was made of leather. "I remember he put his shoulder pads on backwards," Buonocore said.

By the end of the season, Bawza was starting. On the kickoff after New London's latest touchdown, he was the up man. The ball came right to him at the 15 and he took off down the right sideline.

"The guys in front of me leveled everybody," Bawza said. "I wasn't a speedster. I just had to break and shake a little."

He was finally caught from behind, but not until NFA had first-and-goal at the New London 5. Ruffo later scored from less than a yard with 8:08 left in the quarter. Suddenly, NFA had life.

After both teams were stopped—New London on downs twice, NFA on Ritter's fourth interception of the day—the Wildcats got back in gear.

"We figured we'd cruise to another 25 points with no problems," New London's Booth said. "But they wouldn't quit. They scored one touchdown, it was no big deal. Then we didn't score, then they scored and we didn't again."

A 67-yard drive ended with Jakubielski's 35-yard touchdown pass to Eccles. A 37-yard pass to Eccles helped set up John Saporita's 1-yard plunge to make it 25–23 with 16 seconds left in the third quarter.

Eccles was the NFA manager for three years, but he came out for football senior year only after a long, late-night discussion with his parents. He became Jakubielski's favorite receiver.

"I finally decided this was it," he said about coming out for the team. "We stayed up until three one morning talking about it. I think the only reason my mother said yes was because she was tired and wanted to go to bed. She said, 'Go ahead, but you're going to get hurt.' She was right."

Eccles injured his knee on the catch that set up Saporita's touchdown, getting thrown into one of the metal poles that laced cable around the perimeter of the field. But he stayed in the game, and played a crucial role in its dramatic finish.

After Saporita scored, NFA's Arnold "Bubba" French pounced on a Speedwell fumble to give NFA the ball at the New London 13. Ruffo went in from the 3, Jakubielski added the kick and it was 30–25 Wildcats with less than a quarter to go.

The Wildcats had scored 27 straight points.

"We weren't supposed to be that close," Ruffo said. "They were the top team in the state. We just sucked it up and couldn't let it go by that easy."

The mighty Whalers had given up four straight touchdowns and trailed with 10½ minutes left.

"All I was thinking was that this is a great rivalry, this is a great football team and this was going to be a great upset," Weiss said. "Christ, who needs that?"

Brennan then took the Whalers 58 yards, finishing the drive with a 17-yard touchdown pass to Booth. The rushing conversion failed but the Whalers again had the lead, 31–30.

NFA, however, turned around and came back again. *The drive stalled but Jakubielski, a right-handed passer but a left-handed kicker, booted a 32-yard field goal with 4:14 left.*

The kick was actually 42 yards, but at the time the 10 yards in the end zone didn't count in compiling the distance. And Jakubielski had been playing most of the half with his nose continuously bleeding, courtesy of a forearm by Major.

"It was like a spigot," NFA lineman Roland Bennett said.

Teammates say Jakubielski avoided the coaches, who may have pulled him because of the injury. All he remembers is that it wasn't bad enough to take him out.

"I was determined to play, and just keep playing," he said. "Once the adrenaline kicks in, you just keep going."

The Whalers, meanwhile, were stunned. They had trailed only four times all season, and three of them were in this game.

"It was quite hectic," John Brennan said. "We had this big lead and we blew it. I was talking to guys, they were upset. Most of them were crying. I remember going over and saying don't worry about it. Keep cool and we'll score."

The Whalers believed in Brennan. Some also had slightly different recollections of his choice of encouraging words.

"John was a real confident quarterback," Booth said. "He came in the huddle and said, 'We're going to win this game, so shut up.'"

Brennan delivered.

New London went 55 yards in five plays. The fourth play was a pass to Booth, who ran a post pattern and was triple-covered. It was all he could do to bat the ball away and prevent it from being intercepted. The fifth play was to run exactly the same. This time he split two defenders and outraced them to the right corner of the end zone for a 33-yard score.

It was Brennan's five-touchdown pass of the game, his third to Booth. Brennan completed 15 of 28 passes for 271 yards with two interceptions.

"John was a great competitor," Weiss said. "He was a cool kid under pressure. That's not coaching, that's the kid."

The Wildcats were stopped when Tim Lewis intercepted a Jakubielski pass intended for Eccles at the New London 18.

Lewis, a sophomore, got a chance to play because Eccleston had moved to offense and Ritter had left in the third quarter with a broken ankle, suffered on a hit by Ruffo. Before the interception, Eccles had been catching almost everything his way.

"Buonocore was up in the press box," Lewis said. "I think he was picking on me."

But NFA—naturally—wasn't through yet. The Wildcats got the ball back again and Jakubielski (13 of 28, 241 yards, seven interceptions) threw it toward the end zone with 36 seconds left.

What happened after the ball got there is a closed subject to the Whalers. For the Wildcats, however, it is still an object of fierce debate.

And, ultimately, the symbol of anguish and futility in a great comeback never consummated.

With a play set for Bob Bundy on the right side, Jakubielski instead went to the left to Eccles, who again had Lewis on him. They went up for the ball together and were on their way down with the ball together. But when they hit the turf, it was Lewis who had control. Field judge Norm Abell ruled it an interception.

"There was no doubt about it," Lewis said. "It was a long time ago, but I came down with it. I came down with it."

Said Jakubielski: "They say it was intercepted. I still don't believe it until this day. I still see it to this day. That was a simultaneous reception. When guys grab the ball at the same time, it goes to the offensive player."

The Whalers, to a man, agree with Lewis. The Wildcats, except for two, side with Jakubielski.

"It was an interception," Bawza said. "When they came down (Lewis) wrestled it away from Ward. The call could have gone either way, but (Lewis) did have possession."

The other player is Eccles, and he's not talking.

"I've never been asked to this day," he said. "In 25 years, I've never said. I'm not saying now. It was a very close play, there's no need for controversy. One play doesn't make the game."

Eccles will make one point about the play.

"If you ever look at the film," he said, "Bundy is wide open."

The Whalers ran out the clock and earned their fifth straight victory in the series.

"It was tough to see that clock go to zero," Ruffo said. "That hurt."

The New London players celebrated, but mostly the end meant the end of the threat. They were more than happy to get on the bus and escape with the victory.

"We were kind of glad it was through," New London's Maggi said. "It was a long, long game."

"It's too bad for the Norwich kids because they put up such a damned good fight," Weiss said. "It was a good lesson for our kids. To learn a lesson and to have won, you are a very fortunate person."

New London escaped, but the victory haunted the Whalers only days later.

Fighting for the No. 1 spot all season with West Haven—the Whalers had reclaimed it the week before the NFA game—the Whalers lost it again.

While New London struggled against NFA, West Haven rolled over seventh-ranked Jonathan Law 34–0.

New London crushed Fitch 51–0 on Thanksgiving Day to win the CDC crown and make one last bid to wrest away the poll's top spot. But West Haven's 76–6 victory over a hapless Hillhouse team sealed its position as No. 1.

There was talk before the NFA game that if both New London and West Haven finished the season unbeaten, they would play at the Yale Bowl. This was eight years before the Connecticut Interscholastic Athletic Conference began state championship games, and the CIAC and CDC didn't object to the proposed game. But it never came about.

"It was a great rumor," New London's Foye said.

The West Haven team did come up for the New London team banquet that year. Films from both teams' games were watched and the merits of both were argued. "We said we'd play them in the parking lot," Booth said.

That never came about either.

For the Wildcats, the season-ending loss was devastated. "If it finished 25–3, it probably wouldn't have been," Rod Depot said. "But we had a shot to win."

In the clubhouse, the players nursed their wounds and shared their grief. Giordano's postgame talk was quiet and quick.

"There's not much you could say to the kids," he said. "The kids gave it everything they could to come back. The demeanor and tone of the clubhouse...what could you say? I told them it was a great effort, I was proud of them and to hold their heads up."

The following Monday, the school's alma mater, played only after victories, went through the speakers.

Later that week the team watched game film. Buonocore—a New London guy who took over as coach of the Whalers the next season—wept as he saw again how close it had been.

One day the next spring, the film was shown continuously at NFA, with waves of students coming and going all day.

After that, the film was kept under wraps. "We could take any film we wanted," Bawza said. "That film, they would not let out."

Even now, NFA players still want to watch the film and want to know how they can get ahold of it. But even without it, the game is still focused in their minds.

"Even though we lost," Ruffo said, "I wouldn't mind playing that game over again."

THEY SAID IT

I don't think there was a guy who played in that game—and everyone gave their all—who didn't say, "If I had only done one more thing."
— NFA running back Leo Bawza

People have said it's the most exciting game they've ever seen. It must have been an incredible game to watch. But when you're playing, you're thinking of other things.
—New London center Rich Foye

I just remember I was relieved (after the game-saving interception in the end zone). I saw there was 30 seconds left and said, "Thank God."
—New London safety Tim Lewis

I truly believe we were the stronger football team, but they weren't bad.
—New London coach Bob Weiss

It was a great game to watch, to play in, and a privilege to coach in. It's something I'll always cherish for many, many years.
—NFA coach Jim Giordano

I think we put our heart and soul into that game. I always say that group of kids was a super bunch. They've always been, in my mind, one of the best teams I've ever worked with.
—NFA assistant Jim Buonocore

In those days it was the biggest game in town. Everybody came and you knew you had to throw out your best effort. I was proud to be a part of that game.
—NFA tackle Clyde Parker.

Even now, people hear my name and say, "Did you play in that 1968 game?" You wonder how people remember it but when you think it, you say, "Yeah, it probably was one of the best games ever played in this area."
—NFA receiver Ward Eccles.

The idea and point is that if you do give your best, there's nothing to be ashamed of. I don't think anybody is ashamed of losing that game. We played our best and some of us played over our heads.
—NFA guard Roland Bennett

We never felt we were out of it. In a lot of the games [that season] *we were a good, strong steady team and we felt we could do stuff. We just needed some breaks.*
—NFA center/linebacker Tom Bielecki

[The win] *created a sense of accomplishment, yet people weren't walking around with a chip on their shoulders anymore, because someone almost knocked it off.*

—New London guard Ron Maggi

For This One, McPhail Had to Pass

Bob McPhail had what he called "a nice little perch."

While thousands would have to scramble, claw and jostle for a seat to watch the 102nd edition of the Norwich Free Academy–New London game, the nation's oldest high school football rivalry, McPhail had his lined up. He would be working with Dave Connors and Tommy Edwards on WNLC's radio coverage.

The 1968 game, like the others before it, was an exercise in civic and school pride. But this one had much more riding on it. NFA, at 7–2, had its best record in five years. New London was 7–0, ranked first in the state and an offensive and defensive juggernaut.

But McPhail's prized seat must have gone to somebody else. He never saw the game.

His 9-year-old son, Marlin, was the state winner in the Punt, Pass and Kick competition and would be participating in the regional event. It was to be held on Sunday, Nov. 17, at halftime of the New York Giants–Philadelphia Eagles game at Yankee Stadium.

The day before, as the NFA–New London game was starting, the McPhail family drove to New York with the game on the radio. But the signal started to fade in Madison and McPhail pulled the car over on I-95.

The family listened to it into the second half, then McPhail started the car again and pointed toward New York.

Marlin went on to win his division and compete in the national semifinals in St. Louis in December, where he finished third.

And Bob?

There is no question his family came first. "It was a big weekend for my son," said McPhail, who later became athletic director at NFA.

When the McPhails got back from New York, Bob called NFA coach Jim Giordano to find out what happened.

The 1969 New London team won its sixth in a row in the series, 27–15.

All that occurred was NFA came back from a 25–3 deficit to take the lead three times, only to fall short in the last minute. The Whalers held on to win 37–33.

"I must have been the only guy in eastern Connecticut who didn't see the game," he said, 25 years later. "I wish I had been there."

In 1969, a new but familiar face returned to the sidelines. Jim Buonocore, who had excelled for Chapman Tech and, in his senior year of 1951, New London High School, left his assistant coaching job at Norwich Free Academy and returned to his alma mater. For the next thirty years, Buonocore would be the greatest coach in New London football history, leading the Whalers to four state championships and 208 career wins.

Forty-two years after his first game, Buonocore admitted it was strange being on the sidelines, going against the players whom he had coached for the previous three years. But he inherited a terrific team that had a sensational back named Tim Lewis to pick up the slack.

In the November 15, 1969 game, Buonocore's return to Norwich, Lewis was the main factor in a 27–15 win. John DeGange of the *Day* wrote:

The story of the 103rd New London–Norwich Free Academy football game could be told in a just a few words: Tim Lewis passed for two touchdowns and ran for two more.

> *Of the four touchdowns, Buonocore thought the first one, giving the Whalers the initial lead, was the most significant because of its psychological impact.*

NFA starting quarterback Jay Brennan was hurt during the game, and junior Rik Little came in and threw a twenty-five-yard touchdown pass to Gary Bohara. Leo Bawza added a one-yard run, but there was no way to counter Lewis. He threw two touchdowns to Steve Lampkin and also scored on runs of sixty-eight and twenty-three yards.

8
CLOSE CALLS
1970–1979

By the beginning of the 1970s, New London was beginning to look like a team that was going to be a force for a long, long time.

Star players abounded at nearly every position. Quarterback Tim Lewis, a six-foot-one 190-pounder, was a Capitol District Conference first-team pick in 1969. Wayne McKenzie and Brian Walker, the latter a track star, made up the backfield. The receivers had speed with the aptly named Rod Speedwell, Reggie Wheeler and tight end Steve Lampkin.

The lines were huge, with Bob DelPaine (six-two, 225 pounds), Dane Sebastian (six-two, 210 pounds) and John Popa (six two, 220 pounds).

And then there were the linebackers. Tommie Major, whom the *Bulletin* called in its 1970 preview "possibly one of the best defensive players ever in Southeastern Connecticut," was a six-foot-one, 205-pound rock who was an All-CDC pick. Harry Fanolis was steady as well.

The faces weren't so familiar at NFA. Gone from the potent offense of 1969 were quarterback Jay Brennan and running backs Dan Ruffo and Leo Bawza. In their place were such names as Rik Little, Jim Arremony, Joe Gioia and Tom Morosky. There was an up-and-comer in sophomore Jim Justice at halfback.

The biggest change came on the line, as six players graduated in 1969, including Bob Papp, who later would become the commandant of the

This page: The 1970 New London–NFA game. The Whalers won, 26–7, for their seventh straight win over the Wildcats.

United States Coast Guard. Co-captain Mike Lafayette stepped up his play on the line.

By the time November 14 rolled around, New London was 5-1 and on the cusp of a strong defense and offense. This culminated in a seventh straight win.

Dennis Riley of the *New London Day* wrote:

> *NORWICH—When is New London's dominance of the nation's oldest interscholastic sports series going to end?*
>
> *This is a prevalent question today in the wake of the Whalers' 26 to 7 victory over Norwich Free Academy's football team in the 104th game in the inter-city rivalry.*
>
> *Quarterback Tim Lewis, a candidate for all-state honors, scored three touchdowns and passed for another as New London overcame a one-point halftime deficit to gain the victory.*
>
> *It was the seventh straight for New London in the series—a string equaled in modern times only by NFA clubs between 1934 and 1940 when the competition involved New London Bulkeley.*
>
> *New London is 14-4 in the series since New London high was formed in 1951.*
>
> *The win gives New London a 6-1 slate in the Capital District Conference and it can tie for the league crown by besting Fitch on Thanksgiving day.*
>
> *LEWIS PUTS ON SHOW*
>
> *Lewis, who was a key performer in New London's 1968 and 1969 wins, put on a fine show before a crowd of 5,900, at the campus.*
>
> *He scored touchdowns on runs of one yard, one foot and 19 yards. He connected with end Reggie Wheeler from eight yards out for another TD.*
>
> *Norwich had the better of the going during a mistake-filled first half but it couldn't do much after New London moved ahead, 12–7, with 4:50 remaining in the third period.*
>
> *Fine kicking by Len Eckstein kept Norwich bottled up during a good portion of the ball game. He averaged about 40 yards for his efforts.*

Norwich, on the other hand, had trouble with kicking situations, and miscues in this department led to a pair of New London scores.

New London scored with 5:56 left in the first period when Lewis went one yard to cap a 29-yard, five-play drive which developed after a 23-yard NFA punt.

The snap from center on the NFA kicking down was high, and Gary Ledoux's punt was partly blocked.

Lewis, on a fourth down-14 situation, passed to Wheeler who beat Academy defenders for a reception that carried to the one.

NFA bounced back after the New London score and got on the board with 4:56 remaining in the quarter.

Freshman Cook Goes 46 Yards

Freshman Willie Cook went 46 yards on a storybook run for the six-pointer. Greg Sinay converted the placement and NFA had its only lead of the day.

In the third period, New London drove 5 yards in 14 plays after the second half kickoff for the go-ahead touchdown. Lewis scored from inside the one.

Lewis figured in the key play in the drive. With a third and seven position on the NFA 41, Lewis went back to pass and found himself trapped in 15 yards behind the line of scrimmage.

But he broke loose and spotted Steve Lampkin all alone at the Norwich 48 and threw cross-field for a completion. Lampkin ran to the Norwich 22 after the reception.

New London pushed over two touchdowns in the fourth quarter.

One developed after the Whalers took possession on the Norwich ten when Ledoux, readying for a punt, had his knee touch the ground when he reached for a low snap from center.

Lewis connected with Wheeler, over the middle, for the TD on the third play thereafter.

A 63-yard drive produced the Whalers' fourth touchdown and Lewis got it on a 19-yard keeper play with 3:54 to play.

A pass from Lewis to Spencer Lancaster, covering 51 yards and carrying to the Norwich 19, was the big gainer in the drive.

Kent Reyes passed to Mike Hadley for a two-point conversion after the final New London touchdown. Reyes was wide with one placekick, had another blocked and passed incompletely on other conversion tries.

Norwich failed to cash in on its other scoring opportunities including one in the first quarter when Ledoux recovered a New London fumble on the Whalers' 34.

Craig Parker's interception stalled the Norwich bid soon after.

Then, late in the third period, New London held Norwich on a fourth-and-two move at the Norwich ten. Parker and Tom Major tackled Cook on the sweep-option.

Reyes was far short on a field goal try from the 42 with 18 seconds to play.

New London is 8-1 for the overall season while NFA is 5-4 and 4-4 in the CDC.

Score by periods:

New London	*6*	*0*	*6*	*14–26*
NFA	*7*	*0*	*0*	*0–7*

NL—Lewis, 1 run (kick failed)
N—Cook, 46 run (Sinay kick).
NL—Lewis 1 run (kick blocked)
NL—Wheeler 8 pass from Lewis (pass failed)
NL—Lewis, 19 run (Hadley pass from Reyes)

Norwich finished 5-5, while New London earned a 9-1 record in 1970, allowing only 6.8 points per game while scoring at a 31.4-points-per-game clip. Reggie Wheeler finished with ten touchdowns.

But the tide was about to turn.

Game at a Glance: November 13, 1971

Things were looking up for the Wildcats in 1971. Ron Delgado was a mobile quarterback, something that NFA hadn't featured in quite some time. A sprinter on the track team, Delgado was different from the other quarterbacks in coach Jim Giordano's scheme. While Paul Jakubielski,

Jay Brennan and Rik Little were capable field generals, neither was considered a runner.

That all changed for the 1971 season. Eighteen lettermen returned from a season that was beset with injuries, and all were to contribute. Jim Justice also was set to take the reins at halfback, using his five-foot-ten, 170-pound size to his advantage. Swing man Tom Morosky also proved invaluable, as was fullback Joe Gioia. Sophomore Willie Cook was showing flashes of brilliance at receiver.

On the line, big six-foot-three, 230-pound Dan Rose manned one tackle, while six-foot-one, 207-pound Dan Grillo was at the other spot.

Tom Garvie was an All-CDC pick at cornerback, too.

New London was a group of stars, as well, under coach Jim Buonocore, who had gone 16-4 in his first two seasons. Twenty-two lettermen returned to the team, including Kent Reyes, who was asserting himself as a stellar quarterback and more-than-capable placekicker. In 1970, Reyes set the state record with a forty-nine-yard field goal.

Interestingly, there were five brother combinations on the Whalers, including Martin and Eric Olsen and John and Steve Krupa, all on the line. Co-captains Mike Hadley and defensive end Nate Johnson led the way.

So on November 13, this seemed to be a real clash at Veterans Field in New London. Could the Whalers continue their winning streak? Or would the Wildcats eke out a win?

It wasn't even close.

Roger Montgomery of the *New London Day* wrote:

> *New London—Norwich quarterback Ron Delgado leaped into the arms of end Joe Ziemba. Fullback Joe Gioia scrambled to his feet after falling on the last play and spiraled the football skyward. No one cared it landed uncaught near midfield.*
>
> *It was celebration: Norwich Free Academy 34, New London High 14. New London's modern dominance of the nation's oldest high school football rivalry had just faded into Saturday's sun-streaked greyness.*
>
> *The bitter cold of the day and the unexpected Wildcat margin numbed the sellout crowd at Veteran Memorial Field's final 1971 game.*

The Whalers, however, could point to big plays by receiver Ziemba and speedback Willie Cook as their own source of pain.

Of the five Norwich touchdowns Ziemba's run with a Delgado pass immediately after the Whaler score, and Cook's 88-yard kickoff return to start the second half were the plays that drained the Whaler spirit.

"Without those two plays, we'd have been right back in there," Whaler Coach Jim Buonocore confirmed.

And the Whaler coach added, "You know, I don't usually get upset about a game, but I am this time. I just think we're a better club than we showed." He paused and added, "I will say that this was the worst we have looked in my three years at New London."

AGREES ON KEY PLAYS

Norwich Coach Jim Giordano agreed about the key plays. "The Ziemba score was actually designed to be a short pass, but we caught the secondary up close and he slipped behind them and it ended up being 71 yards. We needed the pickup then because new London had just scored."

Of Cook's run, his coach commented, "That was the other big play. When you get that runback after halftime, it takes away from any psychological edge the other team may have picked up in the locker room."

Cook also set up the first Norwich TD by returning a Kent Reyes punt from the Norwich 49 to the New London 27. Eight plays later, Delgado burrowed his way for a one-yard score with 27 seconds to go in the first quarter.

Jim Justice, who combined with Cook to form a rugged running combo for the visitors, plunged four yards for the next Norwich TD midway in the second period. Wildcat guard Ray Congdon set up the score by recovering a Whaler fumble 20 yards from the goal line.

"Our game plan was to stay on the ground," Giordano explained. "We wanted to keep Kent Reyes and company sitting on the bench and make the New London defense play. We felt that was the way to keep them from scoring."

Fumble Starts Drive

The strategy worked perfectly until Craig Parker of New London scooped up a Norwich fumble on the Whaler 23, still on the second period. Quarterback Reyes then constructed a 10-play drive for a score.

Reyes passed to tight end Larry Pemberton for the 29-yard pass-run scoring play. Pemberton, who caught two other passes during the afternoon, played with a swollen knee. He collided with another player in pre-game practice and was carried back to the dressing room. Nevertheless, he played the whole game.

An undeniable factor in the Whalers' poor showing was the injury plague that depleted the secondary. Only Craig Parker started Saturday, of a four-man unit that looked one of the state's best eight weeks ago.

Immediately after Justice returned Reyes' kickoff to the 29, Delgado probed that weakness and found Ziemba behind the NL defenders. No one was within five yards of Ziemba as he caught the ball near the Whaler 35. He ran unmolested the rest of the way.

Still, New London trailed by just two TDs at the half.

"New London is a spooky club," Giordano observed. "They can score and score fast. We needed another."

Then came Reyes' second half kickoff to sophomore Cook. He took it near the right sideline and cut to his left. The wall of blockers formed perfectly, Cook paced himself until he saw a clear field ahead and then changed speeds to outsprint the last NL defender.

Whalers Forced to Throw

With a three-touchdown deficit, the Whalers were forced to start passing. "I think that if we'd had the opportunity we could have established our running game," Buonocore reported. "But we couldn't while we were behind."

The passes didn't work as Norwich intercepted four. Linebacker Jim Leone and deep backs Neil Gilman and Tom Garvie were especially effective on defense.

Gioia took a touchdown pass moments later, after one of the interceptions, for the last Norwich score. "Really, we only passed eight times," Giordano pointed out, "but two were touchdowns. We completed five."

Running back Rod Speedwell of the Whalers returned the last Norwich kickoff 75 yards to the Wildcat nine before being dropped. The Cat defense held then, but Speedwell also ran 24 yards in a final period drive that saw Reyes plunge in from the one with the last score.

"I figure our mistakes contributed directly to three of their scores," Buonocore summed up.

Norwich	*7*	*14*	*13*	*0–34*
New London	*0*	*7*	*0*	*7–14*

N—Delgado, 1 run (Sinay kick)
N—Justice, 4 run (Sinay kick)
NL—Pemberton 29 pass from Reyes (Reyes kick)
N—Ziemba 71 pass from Delgado (Sinay kick)
N—Cook 88 kickoff return (Sinay kick)
N—Gioia 12 pass from Delgado (kick failed)
NL—Reyes 1 run (Reyes kick)

NFA finished 7-2-1 in 1971 and was second in the area with 9.60 points allowed per game all season and third in offense (25.90 points per game). New London, at 7-3, was fourth in the area in offense (22.10) and third in defense (14.80).

In 1972, New London dropped out of the Capitol District Conference to play an independent schedule. It also fell into Class M, based on dropping enrollment numbers at the school.

New London coach Jim Buonocore talks to his team prior to a 1972 game.

Jim Lewis catches a touchdown against NFA in the 1973 game.

That didn't seem to affect the play on the field, as the Whalers finished 8-1 and were the top team in Class M and tenth in the state poll. One of those wins was a 16–7 decision over NFA on November 11 in Norwich. Bob Lancaster caught a twenty-one-yard pass from Kent Reyes to give the Whalers a 7–0 lead, but NFA's Bill Stevens scored on a three-yard jaunt to tie the game heading into the half.

Larry Pemberton put New London ahead for good with a twelve-yard run, and the Whalers tacked on the final points when Jim Justice—who rushed for 107 yards—was tackled in the end zone. Kent Reyes kicked both extra points.

Reyes, Pemberton and Lancaster, along with tackle Steven Carboni and center Cory Belgrade, were gone for the 1973 game, played on November 10 in New London. It was the last game of the rivalry played at Veterans Field, and the Whalers went out in style with a 14–6 win. Jim Lewis—who finished with fifteen touchdowns this season—caught two touchdown passes from quarterback Mike Foye to account for New London's scores. Foye finished with a school-record twenty-three touchdowns and 1,824 passing yards that season. Roger Montgomery of the *Day* wrote:

> *The second TD throw was also for 11 yards in the final period, ending a 46-yard drive. The key play in the series came when Eddie Robinson, the number two NL receiver, took a Foye pass for 14 yards and a crucial first down just two plays before the TD. Steady kicker Tony Serrano booted both extra points.*

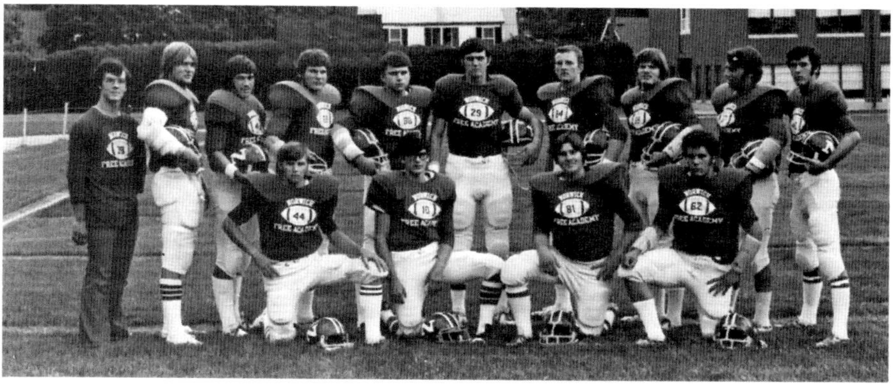

The 1974 NFA seniors. *From left to right, first row*: Martell, McCarthy, Bartha and Leonard. *Second row*: Sanders, Geissler, Boyd, Lafayette, Grillo, Distasio, Abrahamson, Riley, Hamel and Cormier.

New London tri-captain and quarterback Mike Foye in 1974.

Kevin Riley picked off a pass and ran thirty yards for NFA's lone score. The Wildcats were hurt by the loss of eleven lettermen at the start of the 1973 season, including All-CDC performers in running back Jim Justice, tackle Dan Rose, linebackers Jim Leone and Ray Congdon and defensive back Neil Gilman. Despite this, NFA finished 6-3-1 and shared the CDC championship with New Britain, while New London was 8-2 and third in Class M.

In 1974, NFA coach Jim Giordano wanted to open up the offense and began with new quarterback Jim McCarthy. It was going to be tough without the graduated Willie Cook and his nine hundred yards from 1973, but the academy had some capable replacements in Tom Boyd and Robert Jarmon. Tom Distasio made the move from quarterback to halfback.

On November 16, Distasio gave the Wildcats the first bit of good news in their rivalry game by scoring on a one-yard run to give NFA a 7–0 first-quarter lead.

Aside from Don Hazzard's 102 rushing yards, it actually turned out to be the only piece of good news for Norwich.

The Whalers scored the next forty points in a 40–7 win. New London quarterback Mike Foye finished eleven out of twenty-five for 188 yards, and Willie Cook hauled in two touchdowns.

Game at a Glance: November 15, 1975

The 100th anniversary of the first game was played on New London's new field at the high school, to be called Cannamela Field. Despite losing quarterback Mike Foye, who tied his own school record with twenty-three touchdown passes in 1974, to graduation, Kaye Pinhey stepped in and led the Whaler attack with able receivers Reggie Eccleston and Terry Bowens.

NFA, which would be playing its final season in the Capitol District Conference, was full of youth but still featured stalwarts such as offensive guard/defensive tackle Kevin Hamel and fullback Mark Wojtkiewicz. Bob Jarmon excelled in the backfield, and Rich Cipriani played well at receiver.

This page: Photos from the 1975 game, which New London won, 28–7, for its fourth win in a row.

The Whalers, who averaged 22.73 points per game in 1975, were right on target in the centennial game on November 15. Ed Murphy of the *Day* wrote:

> *NEW LONDON—The New London Whalers combined an aerial bombardment with a consistent running attack Saturday and defeated the Norwich Free Academy Wildcats, 28–7, in the 100th anniversary of the oldest schoolboy rivalry in the country.*
>
> *New London coach Jim Buonocore said after the game, "I was really proud of them. They played just the way I wanted them to. It's an honor to coach a team like this."*

Norwich drew first blood in the traditional contest as Paul Robbins charged through the Whaler offensive line and blocked a New London punt. Robbins scooped up the ball at the Whaler 21-yard line and ran in for a 7–0 Wildcats lead.

The Whalers responded by taking the ball after the ensuing kickoff and marching 51 yards to the Norwich one. The drive was capped by Wayne Record's one-yard plunge into the end zone. The Whalers added the point and the score was knotted at 7 with 3:30 remaining in the first quarter.

The Whalers scored again in the second quarter as junior quarterback Kaye Pinhey mixed his passes and runs well and the Whalers marched from the Wildcat 46 to their second score of the game. The drive ended as running back Anthony Major slammed into the end zone, giving New London a 14–7 lead with 7:57 remaining in the half.

The Whalers opened their bag of tricks as they drove for a score in the final minutes of the half. Pinhey completed five passes in the drive. Three, including a 10-yard scoring toss, went to New London's ace receiver, Reggie Eccleston. The scoring pass was completed with 55 seconds left in the half and the Whalers went into the locker room with a 21–7 lead.

Mistakes crushed the Wildcats in the second half as the team moved the ball inside the New London 40-yard line three times, but fumbled the ball over to the hard-hitting New London defense each time.

The Whaler offense also has difficulties in the second half and could not get a sustained drive moving until the final minutes of the contest, when Pinhey began hitting his receivers again.

The final Whaler drive began on their own 37-yard line. The drive was highlighted by a 23-yard completion to Eccleston and a 29-yard completion from running back David Wrighten to receiver Terry Bowens.

The final drive was capped by a 12-yard scoring pass to Eccleston as Pinhey found his talented receiver cutting across the Norwich defense. Pinhey hit him with a perfect pass and the speedy Eccleston outsprinted the defenders to the end zone, making the final score 28–7.

The balanced New London offense moved the ball well most of the afternoon. The Whaler running game amassed 203 yards, while the passing attack totaled 195 yards.

Pinhey completed 12 of 21 passes for 166 yards. He completed six passes to Eccleston for 100 yards and two scores.

Eccleston was also a standout on a defense that allowed the Wildcats only 62 yards passing and 61 yards rushing.

Buonocore said, "There is no question that Eccleston should be all-state, both offensively and defensively."

But, Eccleston is not the only Whaler cited for his performance in Saturday's game. Buonocore said, "We normally give an award to the outstanding back and lineman each game. This week I will be handing out 22 awards in recognition of an outstanding team effort."

This is the fourth year in a row that the Whalers have won the 100-year-old contest. The win brings the current New London record to 6-3-1, while the Wildcats drop to 3-6.

New London	*7*	*14*	*0*	*7–28*
Norwich	*7*	*0*	*0*	*0–7*

N: Robbins, 42 blocked punt (Mitchell kick)
NL: Record, 1 run (Record kick)
NL: Major, 2 run (Record kick)
NL: Eccleston, 10 pass from Pinhey (Record kick)
NL: Eccleston, 12 pass from Pinhey (Record kick)

New London finished 7-3-1 in 1975, while Jim Giordano had his first losing season at Norwich at 3–7.

The 1976 NFA coaching staff, *from left to right*: assistant coach Bob McPhail, assistant coach Paul Giardi, head coach Jim Giordano, assistant coach Merrill Thoresen and trainer John Tedeschi.

New London coach Jim Buonocore meets with Wesley Baldwin during a game.

Everything was new come 1976. The schools played in a new conference—the Southeast Athletic Conference—and for the next five years, they played twice in a season.

Defense was the name of the game for the Wildcats. NFA returned all five defensive line positions: Peter Fargo and Sab Tamborra (ends), Brian Papp and Bill Taylor (tackles) and Mark Campbell (middle guard). The linebacking crew included Mark Ledoux and Randy Bronson, along with Larry Bouley—son of the former Wildcats coach—and Gary Carignan.

The defense played a big role in the first game on September 25. Mark Wojkiewicz scored on a two-yard run to give NFA a 6–0 lead, but New London came right back on Billy Hadley's sixty-nine-yard run. Kaye Pinhey gave the Whalers a 7–6 lead in the second quarter, but NFA drove down and went ahead, 9–6, on quarterback Marlin McPhail's twenty-eight-yard field goal with 1:45 remaining in the first half.

That would be all the scoring in the game, as NFA's defense came through with three interceptions in the fourth quarter. McPhail, who after his high school career became a successful baseball player, finished four of thirteen for 110 yards, and Harold Barber rushed for 84 yards on nineteen carries.

New London got revenge two months later, on November 13, when a series of blocks set the tone. NFA led, 19–6, after three quarters, but the Whalers came roaring back. Kaye Pinhey's one-yard dive and subsequent extra point with six minutes remaining in the contest brought New London to within six points (19–13).

Ed Murphy of the *Day* wrote:

> *The situation now was: If Norwich, which gained 264 yards on the ground all afternoon, could run about seven plays, it would clinch the game. New London, on the other hand, had to come up with its finest defensive effort of the year, use the team's final three timeouts, and force Norwich to punt after three plays.*
>
> *Norwich ran two good plays and had the ball with third down and 4 yards needed for the crucial first down. At this point, the Whaler defense rose to the occasion and dumped Fontaine, who gained 171 yards on 34 attempts on the afternoon, for a 6-yard loss, and forced the Wildcats to attempt the fatal punt with 1:43 remaining.*

Bill Barlow then came through big for the Whalers, blocking the punt. Rich Slocum fell on it in the end zone for a touchdown to tie the score at nineteen. Murphy continued:

> *Whaler coach Jim Buonocore said he did not hesitate to have Pinhey (who was 1-2 on the afternoon) try the field goal extra point.*
>
> *"I saw him kick all week," Buonocore said, "and I knew what he could do—but I must admit, I was holding my breath."*

The kick was good, and New London went ahead for the first time. Norwich had one last chance when McPhail lined up on the Whalers' 25 for a field goal with twenty-nine seconds left, but Bill Hadley burst through the line to block the attempt and save the game for New London.

Norwich got revenge in the first game of 1977, engineering a 70-yard drive in the final minutes of play at Cannamela Field. Bob Fontaine (thirty-eight carries, 224 yards) scored with twenty-three seconds left from 5 yards out to break a 6–6 tie and give NFA the win.

It wasn't over when the final whistle sounded, however. Murphy wrote:

> *Matters, however, did not end there, or even after the final buzzer sounded, ending the game.*

> *At the conclusion of the contest, the ill feelings that often accompany a bitter rivalry replaced the high emotions that kept both sides going through the contest, setting off a bench-clearing, helmet-swinging, punching, kicking brawl.*
>
> *The incident, which was ignited by several off-color comments, ended about five minutes later when order was restored on the field. The only injuries seemed to be to the prides of players who were decked in the scuffle.*

There were no problems in the return game on November 12, except for hurt feelings for New London after a 26–22 loss. Fontaine rushed for 324 yards on thirty-one attempts—he had 1,296 yards through eight games—and scored three touchdowns. Gary Carignan also scored for NFA.

New London made a valiant comeback with two late touchdowns from Billy Hadley (sixty-four yards) and Tim Riordan, but it was too late.

NFA had a new coach for 1978 in Merrill Thoresen, and the teams split again on the field. The Whalers scored twenty-eight straight points in the second half to pull out a 20–14 win, going ahead when Rob Amanti scored on a 24-yard run late in the fourth quarter. Fontaine was injured for Norwich, but his able replacement, Tom Carey, had 221 yards on fifty carries.

One month later, on November 11, Tom Carey scored twice in the first quarter, and Norwich held on for a 26–19 win. Fontaine returned to rush for 199 yards and two touchdowns.

The 1978 New London–NFA game. NFA and New London split the series in 1978. The Whalers won 20–14, while the Wildcats won 26–19.

New London quarterback Lon Pinhey led a sweep in the series in 1979. The Whalers won, 43–12 and 9–6.

Amanti and Lyndon Wrighton scored in the fourth quarter, but New London couldn't get any closer.

The first game of 1979, October 7, was one of the most exciting games of the decade, and it all fell on the shoulders of a kicker who earlier in the game had looked to be the goat.

First, the particulars. After a scoreless first half, the Whalers took a 6–0 lead on Steve Bonneau's thirty-five-yard touchdown pass from Lon Pinhey. The two-point conversion failed.

Tom Perry tied the game for Norwich when he hauled in Andy Lee's forty-two-yard touchdown pass, but the two-point conversion failed, too.

Next came the fourth quarter, and the Whalers were driving late. They were getting into field goal range for George Sabbadini, who had already slumped his shoulders twice after field goal attempts when both missed badly.

Ed Murphy of the *Day* reported:

> *In fact those first two attempts were so far off the mark that fans milling around the sideline openly wondered why Whaler coach Jim Buonocore would be willing to gamble on the young man's foot again.*
>
> *Buonocore said after the game he had no reservations about going with Sabbadini after NFA failed to run out the clock and the Whalers took over the ball on the Norwich 15-yard line with only one second remaining on the clock and the score tied at 6–6.*

> *"He kicks them in practice all the time," Buonocore said. "I knew he could do it."*
>
> *Sabbadini admitted he was nervous as the team went into the huddle before the field goal attempt, but he got some relief when Norwich called a time out in order to let him think about the task a little more.*
>
> *But instead of getting more nervous during that time, Sabbadini used it to settle down.*
>
> *"I was much more nervous before they called the time out," he explained. "I knew what I did wrong on the first two tries and it gave me time to think about correcting those mistakes and think about what I had to do."*
>
> *And when the ball finally was snapped Sabbadini coolly came up and followed through with a perfect kick that split the uprights with about 10 yards to spare.*
>
> *Pandemonium broke out on the New London sideline as the official signaled the kick was good and Sabbadini and most of the other players on the kicking team immediately found themselves at the bottom of a green and gold pig-pile on the 40-yard line.*

Sabbadini's heroics wouldn't be needed on November 12. New London scored twenty-three points in the first quarter, highlighted by Rob Amanti's ninety-two-yard kickoff return, in a 43–12 win. Amanti scored three touchdowns, and Steve Bonneau added two touchdowns, while Ron Shorter had a seventy-yard kickoff return.

The teams ended the 1970s at the opposite of where they had started the decade. NFA was 0-10 in 1979, while New London was 4-5-1.

9
WHALER DOMINANCE

1980–1989

In the *Bulletin*'s 1980 preview, New London coach Jim Buonocore mentioned how there were some "exceptional freshmen" on the team. On the offensive line sat rookies James Scott, Jack Cochran and Dave Berry. Sophomore quarterback Paul Foye followed in the footsteps of his successful brothers Rich (lineman) and Mike (quarterback).

Defensively, the team was strong with Shawn Guess, Chuck Stroneski, Marcus Sanchez and Charlie Green on the line, along with Tom Ferino and Greg Hamler.

For the Wildcats, coach Merrill Thoresen decided to switch things up and go to a Wing-T offense.

When the teams met on September 20, Paul Wojtkiewicz got things started for NFA when he scored on a two-yard run. But New London reeled off nineteen straight points to win 27–12, thanks to Ron Shorter's sixty-four-yard punt return and thirty-seven-yard run. Sam Jones also caught two touchdown passes from Foye.

The Wildcats didn't fare much better in the second game on November 15. Shorter scored on one- and thirty-two-yard runs, and Guess had a thirty-seven-yard interception return for a 21–0 win.

The teams stopped playing twice a year in 1981, which probably was a good thing for NFA. NFA lost, 14–6, when Ron Shorter (172 yards rushing) scored on a 1-yard run and caught a 10-yard touchdown pass from Dan Venditto, both in the second quarter. The win clinched the first Southeast Athletic Conference title for the Whalers in the six-year history of the league. It was the first league title of any kind for New London since the 1970 Capitol District Conference Championship.

The *New London Day*'s Don Cawley wrote:

> *"It's been a long time for us," said Buonocore. "We've had a lot of good teams over the years, but we haven't been able to win a championship."*
>
> *It was obvious from the post-game celebration in the New London locker room that Buonocore's players appreciated the significance of Saturday's victory. There was singing, screaming, clapping and dancing for a good 30 minutes after the game. And Buonocore was loving it. In fact, he showed his players that they weren't the only ones who knew how to shake a leg, moving into the center of a circle of players and demonstrating that the ol' coach has a few disco moves of his own*

Game at a Glance: November 13, 1982

NFA had a number of players who took a lot of lumps over the past three seasons, and something had to give. Enter the 1982 season, the first of the Eastern Connecticut Conference.

The Wildcats had twenty-four seniors on the team who were ready to forget the pain of years past. There also was a new coach, Ed Sweeney, who replaced Merrill Thoresen and introduced a different offense that featured multiple weapons.

The offensive line was stacked with experience, including Jeff Sharpe, Larry Balsley, Mike Blanchette, Ed Tamborra and Doug Jakobik. Todd Clairwood was a rock at nose guard. Chris McNally led the linebacking corps, and Mike Delucia guided the secondary.

It culminated in a 6-3 record, including something that hadn't happened since the 1977 season: a win over New London.

Under the *Bulletin*'s headline "Bombs Away, It's NFA," Bill Toscano wrote:

Norwich—Norwich Free Academy's football turnaround became complete yesterday.

And it happened on one play.

With one second left in the first half, the Wildcats, the same team that was 1-9 last season and 1-29-1 over the last three, held a respectable 14-2 lead over New London and had the ball at their own 35-yard line.

NFA called time out and Brian Mignault, the Acads' offensive coordinator, pulled a play they call "bombs away" out of the playbook.

Three receivers split out to the right side of the field and took off when the ball was snapped. With fans expecting him to simply fall on the ball, NFA quarterback Andy Lee dropped back and lofted a "Hail Mary" pass to split end Mike Bean, who was streaking across the Whalers' 35-yard line.

But as has always happened over the last few years, the ball bounced off the NFA receiver's arms, off his chest and tumbled backward toward the ground.

Last year, or the year before that, the ball would have rolled end-over-end across the turf, and the half would have ended and New London might very well have had a chance to come back.

Not this year.

Instead of hitting the ground, the ball fell right into the waiting hands of junior running back Steve Lee, who hugged it and scampered into the end zone, giving Norwich a 20–2 lead which stood as the final score.

"The ball landed in my hands—I mean right in my hands; I didn't even have to move them," Lee said. "It usually happens the other way."

What made the miracle play and the win that much more satisfying was that it came over New London, a team that has beaten the Acads twice a year for the last four years in the continuation of the nation's oldest high school football rivalry.

This year, playing the Whalers only once made it mean that much more, said tri-captain Chris McNally.

"Losing the SAC and double-scheduling, we learned what the rivalry was all about," the senior middle linebacker said after Norwich won the 121st game between the two schools. "It's a one-shot deal. You don't get two times to play the game.

"You've got a lot going for you in this game," Norwich coach Ed Sweeney said. "We're rivals, our seniors had never beaten this team, it was Homecoming and we had to bounce back from last week."

Norwich had something else going for it yesterday, something the Wildcats hadn't been getting consistently this season—a solid offensive performance.

"Our coaches emphasized all week that the offense is the key to everything we've got," said Norwich quarterback Andy Lee, who connected on five of 10 passes for 85 yards, including the 65-yard touchdown pass on the last play of the first half. "We went right at them and I think that's the only way to beat New London."

New London coach Jim Buonocore, whose team dropped to 5-4, said Norwich simply did what it had to do.

"They moved the ball on our offense and they stopped us when they had to," Buonocore said after seeing one of his teams lose its third straight game for the first time ever.

Norwich's offense, which rolled up 294 yards, scored the first two times it touched the ball and controlled the ball well in the second half to put the game away.

In fact, that second half featured solid performances from a number of young players like sophomore Rick Deschamps, who ran for 59 yards, junior John Brophy who had 32 yards and sophomore Darryl Benoit, who ran for 18 yards.

"We were psyched all week with the tradition," said junior guard Tim Ouellet, part of the NFA offensive line that controlled the line of scrimmage, gave Lee time enough to pass and opened holes for the Wildcats' backs.

"We sustained our blocks, had leg drive and fired out," Ouellet continued. "We let our running backs run. That's all we had to do."

Norwich took the opening kickoff on its own 30-yard line and drove 70 yards in 10 plays to take an 8–0 lead with 5:34 left in the first quarter.

Nine of those plays were runs by Steve Lee, who scored on a one-yard plunge. Lee, who suffered a hip injury in the third quarter, wound up with 101 yards on 19 carries. The other play in the drive was an 11-yard pass from Andy Lee to Mike DeLucia. That same duo hooked up on the conversion. Norwich was also helped along by 25 yards in penalties against the Whalers.

New London had some trouble moving the ball on its first possession and on the sixth play of that drive, defensive end Todd Murphy recovered a fumble giving Norwich the ball on the Whaler 47.

Eight plays later, on the first play of the second quarter, Deschamps bulled over from the one to make it 14–0. That touchdown was set up on a 15-yard hook and ladder pass from Andy Lee to DeLucia to Steve Lee.

New London couldn't move on its next possession and the third and fourth times the Whalers had the ball, their drives ended with Norwich interceptions deep in Wildcat territory.

With 2:53 left in the first half DeLucia picked off a Foye pass on the Norwich one-yard line.

Norwich couldn't move the ball either, and when Steve Lee lined up in his own end zone to punt, the snap was bad, so he wisely ran out of the end zone, giving New London its only two points of the game.

New London linebacker John Green ran back the ensuing free kick to the Norwich 3, but four plays later, Bruce Maynard intercepted Foye in the end zone and ran it out to the 20-yard line.

Two runs by Deschamps moved the ball to the 35, the clock showed one second and as Andy Lee dropped back, the sun finally came out and shone on the Wildcats.

For all the good feelings that win gave the Wildcats, the loss of those twenty-four seniors hurt. And it would hurt for a long, long time.

The year 1983 saw the first in what would become a staple of New London coach Jim Buonocore's teams: a state championship. The Whalers were stacked—were they ever! Senior tri-captain Dan Venditto returned as quarterback and had six players who could carry the ball: Paul Howard, Dwayn Williams, Rick Miller, Leon Owens, Mark Penaflor and John Pickering. Senior tri-captain Jack Cochran—the class president—could catch anything at tight end. Juan Roman anchored the offensive line and linebacking positions. On defense, George Ellis and Travis Goode, along with Cochran and Lynn Crisler, saw time on the line. The defense was the strong point.

Right: The 1983 tri-captains Dan Venditto, Juan Roman and Jack Cochran with coach Jim Buonocore.

Below: The 1983 New London team won its first CIAC state championship and became the first New London team to finish a season 11-0.

Buonocore said early in the season that he wanted to get off on the right foot. A 48–6 win over Stonington was a great start.

The wins continued to pile up: 17–0 over Bishop Hendricken of Rhode Island, 6–0 over Waterford (in which Howard scored the lone touchdown on a sixty-one-yard punt return) and 31–13 over Montville, as well as shutouts over Killingly (27–0) and St. Bernard (14–0).

When the 8-0 Whalers met the 5-3 Wildcats on November 12, New London kept right on rolling. Williams scored two touchdowns, Venditto added another and New London won, 21–6.

A few weeks later, New London beat Torrington, 24–0, in the Class M championship game for its first state title since the current playoff system was introduced in 1976. The Whalers finished 11–0.

New London kept rolling into 1984, going unbeaten in its first six games before a 29–14 loss to Ledyard on October 27. Two weeks later,

Leon Owens's seven-yard third-quarter touchdown and Jon Hargrove's extra point were all the Whalers needed for a 7–0 win at Norwich.

Sweeney stepped aside after the '84 season in which the Wildcats went 1-7-1, and Brian Mignault became the new coach at NFA. The Wildcats had exceptional backfield speed with Floyd Overton at quarterback, along with running backs John Newson and Tony Nelson. NFA earned one more win in 1985, but it didn't come against its longtime rival.

New London eked out a 20–14 win on two touchdown passes from Victor Ebersole to Hector Aquino. James Smith also hauled in a touchdown pass that provided the difference in the Whalers' third straight win.

A new player came on the scene for New London in 1986. In his first varsity game against Plainville, on September 13, Jamal Johnson scored two touchdowns on runs of thirty-two and twenty-two yards. These were the first two scores in a career that ranks among the best ever in eastern Connecticut.

The Whalers were 5-3 heading into their game with Norwich, which continued to stumble at 2-7. The offense eluded the Wildcats on November 15 as the Whalers won, 20–0. Johnson hauled in a twenty-two-yard pass from Smith, while Todd Fine caught two touchdown passes—one each from Johnson and quarterback Kevin Lynch.

Johnson continued to stand out in 1987—as did the Whalers. In the first game of the season, his ninety-two-yard kickoff return accounted for New London's only score in a 7–6 win at Plainville, and the Whalers kept on winning. They were 3-0 when they faced NFA on October 10; NFA was 0-3. Predictably, New London won, 45–7. Johnson had scoring runs of sixty-one and thirty yards and returned an interception six yards for a third score. Courtland Hall also had an interception return.

The Whalers kept right on winning, all the way to the Class S championship game—where they lost to Ansonia, 28–27, to finish 10-1. Johnson scored sixteen touchdowns that season.

Game at a Glance: October 9, 1988

Jamal Johnson was one of the greatest running backs in New London history. *Courtesy of the* New London Day.

New London made sure to show that 1987 was no fluke. Johnson returned for his senior season, and linemen Ed Samul and Jason Appleby made sure to keep the holes open for Johnson, who would rush for more than three thousand yards in his career.

NFA, meanwhile, continued to struggle under Mignault, coming off a 2-8 1987 season. The Wildcats were young but had an up-and-coming star in quarterback/defensive back Jemal Davis.

New London again came into the rivalry game on October 8 with a 3-0 record, while the Wildcats were 1-2. This time, it was Johnson's time to shine.

Under the headline "Whalers' Domination Continues," *Bulletin* reporter Jim Konrad wrote:

> *Norwich—Give Jamal Johnson an inch, and he'll take a yard. Or 30. And six points to boot.*
>
> *New London's standout tailback rushed for 207 yards and two touchdowns and returned a fumble for another score yesterday as the Whalers defeated Norwich Free Academy 24–0 in the continuation of the nation's longest high school football rivalry.*
>
> *That rivalry has turned one-sided, with the Whalers winning the last six games, and 10 of 11 in the '80s.*
>
> *In less historic terms, the Whalers, ranked seventh in the state coaches poll, are 4-0 overall, 2-0 in the Eastern Connecticut Conference Yankee Division. NFA is 1-3, 0-2.*

Johnson (30 carries) did most of the damage in yesterday's rousting in a constant drizzle. His scoring runs of 48 and 31 yards gave him seven rushing touchdowns this season, with an average length of 30 yards each. He has nine TDs overall, including a 42-yard pickup of a fumble in the fourth quarter yesterday.

"You have to hit him high and wrap your arms around him," NFA linebacker Matt Jacobson said. "You can't arm tackle him. You have to keep hammering. That's a big part of it. And you can't do it when he's in the (defensive) backfield."

The first touchdown came just five plays into the game, with Johnson going off right tackle, making a quick hesitation and blowing down the sideline untouched.

Johnson had 147 yards on 22 carries in the first half and the Whalers got inside the NFA 20 three times. But Johnson fumbled, NFA's Jemal Davis picked off a Todd Eukel pass in the end zone and New London lost the ball on downs. The Wildcats didn't cross midfield and it remained 6–0 at intermission.

"We were just too anxious to get started," New London coach Jim Buonocore said. "That's what slowed us down. We should have taken it piece by piece, instead of trying to get the whole cake."

Jason Appleby took a big bite out of the Wildcats three minutes into the second half. An NFA punt snap went low and Dave Giesing had to track down the ball before booting it into Ed Samul. Appleby fell on the ball in the end zone to make it 12–0.

Johnson added his 31-yard run later in the quarter. In the fourth, he picked Davis' option pitch off the ground and went 42 yards for the final score with 11:19 left. All of New London's conversions—a kick attempt and three passes—failed.

The Whalers had 269 total yards, all but 11 on the ground. The Wildcats had 138 total yards, 122 rushing.

"We're the type of team that has to control the ball," NFA coach Brian Mignault said. "We weren't able to. We let New London control it, and when they do they're very dangerous."

Two weeks later, against Ledyard, Johnson rushed for 427 yards—the fifth-highest total in Connecticut history. Johnson finished with 1,922 yards, twenty-two touchdowns and 145 points in his senior season. The Whalers again went undefeated in the regular season, but a familiar foe was waiting in the Class S championship game: Ansonia. And once again, Ansonia had their number, winning 20–15.

Season at a Glance: 1989

Despite NFA's struggles, Davis proved to be a shining light. He was the perfect option quarterback—able to run with zeal or throw with accuracy. He also stood out as a defensive back, a position that would later land him in Storrs to play for the University of Connecticut.

Interestingly, Davis was born in New London and spent most of his youth there before moving to Norwich as a young teen. On September 15, 1989, Greg Reid of the *Bulletin* wrote a profile of the athlete who, nearly twenty years later, would become head coach of his alma mater:

> *Norwich—Of course Norwich Free Academy quarterback Jemal Davis loves to run the option.*
>
> *Making the most of his options was a Davis trademark long before he claimed the No. 1 jersey from the uniform rack or started giving an interception return more stops and starts than a postal route.*
>
> *"In order for me to contribute, I have to have the ball in my hands," Davis says. "With the option (offense), I get to decide whether to give the ball to the fullback, pitch it back or take it myself. The biggest decision is figuring out what to do and when to do it."*
>
> *Entering his second year as the Wildcats' starting quarterback and his third year at free safety, Davis has proven he's pretty good at making decisions.*
>
> *Last season Davis had a hand in scoring 58 of NFA's 106 points.*
>
> *As quarterback he ran for three touchdowns, threw for three more and completed five two-point conversions. He added two more TDs on punt and interception returns.*

And, as an 18-year-old senior, Davis seems to realize that the choices ahead will be more important than deciding which hole to hit. He's known that for a long time.

"I'd still go to college even if there wasn't the chance (of earning a football scholarship)," Davis says. "Football would just determine what type of school I'd go to, like a bigger or smaller one. The important thing is to go to a good school and get good grades."

That decision wasn't made last season, when he picked off 10 passes and was named All-Eastern Connecticut by the Bulletin *and All-Eastern Connecticut Conference. It wasn't made with the arrival of recruiting letters from colleges such as Syracuse, Boston College and even Nebraska.*

The decision to go to college was made in 1987, after Davis' freshman year at Norwich Tech.

"Jemal gave that year to me," his mother Paula says. "I'm a single, working parent and at the time I didn't think we could afford college. I wanted Jemal to have a trade."

Though studying drafting interested Davis, he decided he wanted to go to college. But that required a course load that met college requirements.

"One thing I'm very proud of is Jemal doesn't make many rash statements," Paula Davis says. "He says he wants to do something and he takes steps to do it."

Jemal transferred in as a sophomore and became our starting free safety and he played a lot of running back," NFA coach Brian Mignault says. "Then at the start of last year, he initiated the move to quarterback. I've found that players perform better at positions they're happiest at."

NFA senior Ed Gleason sees the results first hand.

"Jemal always seems to come up with the big run," he says. "He's got the speed, the moves to go for 60 or 70 yards at a time. He's the leader of the whole team."

Says Davis: "At tailback, it's up to someone else whether you get the ball or not. Playing quarterback, it's like a general-ship. You have control over how much you can contribute."

Davis' knack for making good decisions might have started at home. Back in 1970, young Paul Davis was thinking of how life might change for blacks in the United States, and how to make life easier for her newborn son.

"I was attending a lot of Black Power meetings and I wanted my child to grow up proud of being black," she says. "I named him Jemal Christopher so he had both a Muslim and a Christian name. I didn't know what the world would be like. I don't go to church every Sunday, but I have a very strong belief in God."

And Paula Davis realized the challenges of raising a child alone in New London's Jefferson Gardens. She decided to move to Norwich in early 1981.

"It was a very tough neighborhood," she says. "I'm glad we left when we did because it's probably worse now, with drugs and everything."

With the 1989 high school season at hand, Davis, at 6-foot, 160 pounds, knows he needs to play well after getting notice that includes preseason all-state mention from the New Haven Register.

Boston College considers Davis among the top high school players in New England, but rates him a step below the Eagles' "1" list. Davis might need a super season if he hopes to play above the Division I-AA level.

That doesn't change much for him.

"I play because it's fun and I like to show that you don't have to be a big guy to hit hard," Davis says. "I just play hard and don't think much about (scouts) during games. If you do, you're bound to mess up."

Says his mother: "It's important for him to go to a college where they help him reach his fullest potential and help him meet the goals he wants to meet. Fortunately, he's good enough at (football) to hopefully use it to get an education."

Davis, a second honors student the last two years at NFA, thinks he'd like to be a lawyer. Or a sportscaster. Or an architect.

"I want to keep a lot of doors open," he says. "If something doesn't work out, you have something to fall back on."

The old option play.

On October 7, the 3-1 Wildcats faced the 4-0 Whalers. A game that featured much pregame hype didn't turn out that way in the end for NFA. The *Bulletin*'s Peter Abraham wrote:

The New London–Norwich Free Academy football game continued the oldest high school rivalry in the nation.

But it also continued a disturbing trend for the Wildcats—domination at the hands of the Whalers.

NFA, supposedly fielding its best football team in years, was little match for the Whalers yesterday, falling 32–6.

The Eastern Connecticut conference Yankee Division game was the 128th meeting between the schools and capped a decade that will be remembered for New London's dominance.

The Whalers (4-0, 2-0) won 11 of 12 in the 1980s, including the last seven. NFA has been outscored 121–13 the last four games.

A crowd of about 1,500 watched the Whalers gain 377 yards and win their 24th consecutive regular-season game. NFA (3-1, 1-1) managed only seven first downs.

"We got beaten by a better football team," NFA coach Brian Mignault said. "I can't point to one play or one call or anything like that. They just physically beat us."

Senior quarterback Todd Eukel was the biggest of New London's many heroes. He completed 9 of 14 passes for 205 yards and three touchdowns. He also ran 3 yards for a score in the fourth quarter.

Starting safety Jimmy Buonocore, son of the New London coach, keyed a defense that completely shut down the Wildcats.

NFA quarterback Jemal Davis completed 1 of 17 passes, was intercepted five times and fumbled once. The Wildcats, who came into the game averaging 29 points, gained only 146 yards.

Davis' 90-yard kickoff return against New London's reserves gave NFA its only points with 5:49 left in the game.

"Everybody talked about NFA's offense before the game," said Buonocore, who intercepted one pass and broke up two. "That just got our defense pumped up. My job was containing Davis, but I didn't have to. Our defensive line was all over him."

Davis, pressured by ends Will Ellis and Willie Klinefelter, never got his option game going. Domingos Gomes rushed for 94 yards but also fumbled on the New London 21 for one of NFA's seven turnovers.

"Jemal was being chased five yards back before even had time to think," Mignault said. "Their linemen were so quick off the ball."

Eukel, however, had all day to throw. His 44-yard TD pass to Leo Clinton stunned NFA three minutes into the game.

Eukel's 29-yard pass to Troy McKelvin set up Shea Sanders' 3-yard scoring run with 8:09 left in the first half. With 26 seconds left, Eukel hit Paul Winston for a 13-yard TD.

"We have too many guys to stop," Eukel said. "I have three good receivers and two great backs to get the ball to. I think NFA didn't know who to cover and we took advantage of that."

Sanders and Kevie Durham combined for 144 yards rushing. Winston caught four passes for 50 yards, Clinton two for 56.

New London's best play came in the third quarter. On second down and three at the New London 36, NFA blitzed. But Eukel dumped a short screen pass to Sanders. He raced 64 yards down the left sideline for the score.

"That was the first screen pass we threw this year," New London coach Jim Buonocore said. "It was a good example of the kind of team we have this year, everybody did their job."

Said Sanders: "We want to win the ECC, keep our streak going and get back in the (CIAC) playoffs. The oldest rivalry stuff isn't our biggest concern. But when we're old it'll be nice to remember how well we played in such a big game."

For the third straight season, New London finished the regular season undefeated. Shea Sanders continued the trend of Whaler backfield prowess by leading the area with 124 points. Jim Buonocore's son, Jimmy, was a successful kicker. Leo Clinton and Paul Winston hauled in many of Todd Eukel's passes for scores.

Fortunately for the Whalers, they moved up to Class SS and faced Stratford in the championship game. There, New London won its first title since 1983 with a 29–14 win to finish 11-0.

By far and away, New London was the team of the 1980s in eastern Connecticut. The Whalers went 79-24-3 (.759), finishing ahead of Putnam (68-31-1) and Montville (63-36-1). Norwich headed the other way, finishing at the bottom of the fourteen-team list at 31-67-2 (.320).

10
STREAKS GALORE
1990–1999

With such a gaudy winning percentage, New London coach Jim Buonocore naturally heard from plenty of critics during his time. The *Bulletin*'s Dave Davis made note of this in a September 14, 1990 article:

> *New London—If you're a high school football fan in eastern Connecticut, you've heard the rumors.*
>
> *New London football. Sure they win, but at what expense?*
>
> *Do any of the players graduate? Doesn't coach Jim Buonocore let ineligible players suit up and take the field?*
>
> *Ask Buonocore those questions and all you'll get is a hearty laugh.*
>
> *"I've heard them all," the 22nd-year coach said. "The most common one is that the kids aren't eligible."*
>
> *One thing that can't be denied is the success of the program. The Whalers were 79-24-3 during the 1980s.*
>
> *There were five state title appearances, including championships in 1983 and 1989. And the Whalers have swept the Eastern Connecticut Conference Yankee and Nutmeg division titles in each of the last three seasons, having won 30 straight regular-season games.*
>
> *But is there any merit to the rumors?*

"Sometimes it does get ridiculous," said Buonocore, whose career record is 146-64-7. "And a lot of the things said do bother me. I feel sorry when the kids get put down, because they work hard for what they achieve. It hurts the most when people tell me I'm using the kids."

The New London players, even the New London coaches, aren't always choirboys.

New London kids like to talk to opponents before, during and even after a game. Psych job, intimidation, whatever—it works. Maybe some don't like it. But it is New London's style.

And do all the kids graduate? New London teachers say the school is no worse than others.

"I stay after kids unbelievably," said Buonocore. "The first five weeks (of school) I'm checking on who's getting warning slips. I can be a pain in the butt, but I'm trying to help the kids out.

"My wife (Candace) will help tutor the kids too," Buonocore said.

Candace Buonocore is department head of the Chapter One reading program in the New London school system.

Jamal Johnson, the Whalers all-state running back, finished his career with the Whalers in 1988 but didn't graduate with his class the following June.

Buonocore helped get Johnson into Nassau Community College in Garden City, NY, where Johnson had a chance to get his high school diploma and eventually become eligible to play football.

Johnson left school and never played a down of college football. That is a negative people have used against the Whalers. How could a kid with that much talent not make it?

"Everything was done for him," said Buonocore. "I guess he just didn't want it bad enough. He had the opportunity and went to one of the better junior colleges on the East Coast. That was strictly his decision."

Art Lamoureux, the St. Bernard coach and a New London native, knows Buonocore well. And he's been privy to the innuendos about the Whalers.

"I know Jimmy Buonocore because I coached Babe Ruth Baseball with him," Lamoureux said. "I know the time he spends washing uniforms—by himself. I know the time he spends collecting ads—by himself. I know the times he tries to hustle people to support the program—by himself.

"And I see all the success he's had and I relate that solely to Jimmy Buonocore. And Jimmy Buonocore has been able to establish a football staff around him that is extremely competent and qualified. That's a great football environment for any kid to grow up in."

St. Bernard will play the Whalers Sept. 22 at New London. It's the first time the schools have met since 1983.

"We play against that type of football in the (All Connecticut Conference) every week," said Lamoureux. "And it's great to come back here and play against that."

Buonocore's coaching staff may be his greatest asset.

Gil Varjas and Joe McNeil have been with Buonocore since 1969, when he became head coach. The list of others who have coached under Buonocore reads like a who's who coaching directory: Larry Keating, Bob Nenna, Tom Major, Jack Cochran, Tom Riordan, Reggie Eccleston, Larry Croxton, Tim Lewis, Joe Basilica, Luis Martinez and countless others.

"We all get along," said Buonocore. "We don't have to sit down and discuss a lot of things. Nobody has to come to me for approval.

"I delegate the responsibility very easily. When you work with guys you tell them what you want, but let them do it their way. By letting them coach it the way they want, they feel like it's a part of them. And that's important because they put a lot of time in."

Lamoureux respects New London football. He gives it the highest compliment an opposing coach can: "Say what you want about New London, but don't ever say that it's not a great football program. I want to beat them; that's good football."

There was nothing controversial once New London and NFA met because the Whalers continued to hold the upper hand. The teams met on October 6 in Norwich in the first game of the 1990s, and the Whalers used an eighty-five-yard kickoff return by Kevin Graham to pull out a 21–12 win. New London finished the season 8-2. Norwich went 5-4 for its first winning season since 1982. But that would be as good as it got for the Wildcats.

New London was 8-0 and running over everyone when it hosted 2-4-1 NFA on November 9. The Whalers scored twenty first-quarter points en route to a 40–6 win; running back Ambrose Fletcher scored two touchdowns on the ground, and receiver Troy McKelvin hauled in two scores from John Mikula. Ambrose's brother, Kasi, also got into the act with a thirty-yard touchdown catch from Mikula and a twenty-eight-yard run.

The Whalers finished 11-0 in the regular season and faced noted nemesis Ansonia in the Class S championship game. But the third time was the charm for New London; the Whalers ran away with a 34–18 win for their third state championship.

The Fletcher brothers helped keep the good times going in 1992. Once again, New London was 6-1 in meeting 2-5 NFA on November 7 in Norwich. This time, the Whalers' defense stepped up with a 37–0 whitewashing. Joe Bustamante caught two touchdowns from Tom Faraci, and Ambrose Fletcher ran for three scores.

The Whalers finished the regular season 10-1—their lone loss a 10–7 defeat against Ledyard the week before the NFA game—and again faced Ansonia in the Class S championship. New London exorcised the demons for the second straight year, pulling out a 21–19 win that featured a seventy-six-yard run from Ambrose Fletcher.

NFA continued to fall behind, but new life was breathed into the program with the hiring of Steve Robichaud as coach for the 1993 season. Robichaud had spent time as an assistant in the early 1990s with UConn, and when coach Tom Jackson stepped down, Robichaud needed a place to go with his young family.

NFA coach Steve Robichaud in 2001. Robichaud brought the Wildcats to new heights in the late 1990s and early 2000s. *Courtesy of the* Norwich Bulletin.

Enter Norwich Free Academy. Brian Mignault (and later, John Robinson) stepped down as coach, and Robichaud went for the opening.

In 1993, the Wildcats continued to take their lumps, winning just one game out of six heading into the November 6 matchup with New London. The Whalers had cooled off their run as well, being only 3-4 at the same point.

It didn't matter.

The Whalers racked up thirty-one points in the second half to win, 51–18, at Cannamela Field. Aaron Hairston scored three times, Bustamante hit a thirty-seven-yard field goal, five extra points and returned a fumble thirty-two yards to increase the winning streak to twelve games. Ben Schreiner scored twice for the Wildcats, who couldn't overcome a two-point halftime deficit.

Norwich continued to struggle in 1994, standing at only 1-6 on November 5 when New London was at 7-0. New London's Damien D'Angelo threw two touchdowns, and Demond Hastings scored on a seventy-five-yard run to help the Whalers to a 29–2 thrashing.

New London seemed destined for the state playoffs at 8-0, but losses in the final two games doomed its playoff hopes.

The teams began play in September 1995 in the second game of the season. Robichaud's NFA squad began to show the fruits of working hard—as well as a standout player named Major Williams—but the Whalers still had the upper hand, winning 20–14. Nick Gray's three touchdowns proved to be the difference for New London, while Williams (two extra points) and Travis Lanier scored touchdowns for NFA.

The teams opened the season in 1996 with New London winning its fourteenth in a row, 20–6. Izell Malloy ran for two scores, and Gamaliel Perkins added a five-yard run for the Whalers' scores.

And in 1997, when New London raced out to a 19–0 halftime lead, it seemed the fifteenth straight win was well in hand.

Or was it?

Game at a Glance: September 13, 1997

NFA hadn't had a winning season in a decade, but Robichaud had worked his players hard and finally received some talent, too.

Sure, there was Major Williams, a bull of a running back who also featured a strong foot. There was speedy Bryant Stone. Kevin Green had able hands. The defense played well, too.

Optimism abounded in Norwich, and for good reason. New London was coming off a down year.

On September 13, the teams squared off to open the season. Standing on the sideline, the *Bulletin*'s Peter Abraham probably had his story written in his head come halftime.

But that all would change:

> *New London—Some of the players on the Norwich Free Academy sideline on Saturday weren't born the last time the Wildcats beat New London in a football game.*
>
> *It had been that long—1982 to be specific—since the oldest high school rivalry in the country meant something more than a day of frustration and disappointment for NFA.*
>
> *But the Wildcats shed their inglorious past in fine fashion, scoring 20 points in the final 14:17 to stun the Whalers 20–19 at Cannamela Field.*
>
> *Quarterback Major Williams scored two touchdowns for NFA and kicked the decisive extra point with 4:10 left in the game.*
>
> *"I'm not going to say this game means we've turned it around, but it is a great, great win for us," said fourth-year NFA coach Steve Robichaud, who enjoyed a bucket of cold water dumped on his back in the final seconds. "I couldn't be prouder of a group of kids."*
>
> *Many believed this would be the year NFA would finally break through. But for the better part of three quarters the Wildcats ran in place as New London took a 19–0 lead.*
>
> *One play turned the game. New London gambled on fourth-and-three from the NFA 36 in the third quarter, having quarterback Jon Fitzpatrick try for the first down on a bootleg play. Williams, coming from the secondary, beat several blockers and cut Fitzpatrick down for a 6-yard loss.*
>
> *"We never got it back after that," said Whalers coach Jim Buonocore, who admitted he wished he punted. "They had the momentum and we ran out of gas. But that's no excuse."*

Williams capped the next two NFA possessions with touchdowns, scoring from 29 yards out then on a 1-yard sneak.

The momentum shift emboldened the Wildcats' defense. NFA held New London to 19 yards in the second half—two in the fourth quarter.

The Whalers lacked diversity on offense, throwing only three passes. Senior Gamaliel Perkins, who rushed for 94 yards and a touchdown in the first half, gained only 17 yards on 11 carries in the second.

"That was the key, shutting them down," senior safety Kevin Green said. "The defense made it possible."

NFA tailbacks Jeremy Andruskiewicz (21 carries, 79 yards) and Bryant Stone (9 carries, 78 yards) banged away at the exhausted New London defense until Stone burst up the middle for a 26-yard touchdown with 4:10 left.

Stone, a junior, pointed to the end zone as he ran toward it. The seemingly innocent gesture drew a 15-yard penalty for excessive celebration and NFA was forced to try the extra point from 35 yards away.

Williams nailed it.

"I just tried to block it out and kick like I normally do," Williams said. "I knew it was a big kick but I couldn't think about it."

Said Robichaud: "That's a chip shot for him. Buddha makes them from 40 yards in practice all the time. Everybody knew he could do it."

New London had the ball twice more. The first possession ended on downs with 1:42 left when Green broke up a pass. The second ended when Stone made an interception with 1:17 to go.

"It's an incredible feeling," NFA senior lineman Nick Kapilotis said. "Everybody knew we hadn't beaten New London in such a long time. It's special to be part of the team that finally did it."

With the loss, New London trails the series, 65-61-11. But you get the feeling it won't be another 15 years before NFA wins again.

"We've made strides every year," senior tackle Chris O'Neil said. "We played pretty poorly in the first half but we came out a different team in the second half. We knew we could do it and we went out and did it."

Just like that, the tide had turned.

New London football coach Ed Sweeney (left) gets a football helmet from athletic director Jim O'Neil during a press conference in 1998. Sweeney also coached NFA in the early 1980s. *Courtesy of the* Norwich Bulletin.

Brimming with confidence—especially after an 8-3 season—NFA won the 1998 contest 28–7 on September 26, to improve to 2-0. Stone scored twice, and Williams had an eighty-eight-yard punt return to help the Wildcats to a 9-1 regular season and a trip to the CIAC playoffs for the first time in school history.

NFA's season ended in the Class L championship game, 54–26, to Southington, but Robichaud had his team playing at a high level—just as New London had done at the beginning of the decade.

That year also saw the end of one of the greatest coaching performances in state history. After suffering through the team's third straight losing season (4-5-1), Jim Buonocore decided to retire after thirty years and four state championships. He amassed a 208-95-8 won-loss record from 1969 to '98, and his win total was eleventh best in state history as of 2011.

A familiar face stepped in for New London in 1999 in Ed Sweeney, who nearly twenty years earlier, in 1982, had guided NFA to a memorable season. But there would be no magic this time.

The Whalers ended the decade by going 1-9 in 1999, which including a 24–13 loss to NFA on October 16. New London held a 13–12 lead after the first quarter, but NFA, on the strength of Alan Oullette's eighty-five-yard kickoff return and two touchdowns from quarterback Josh Adamec, pulled out a 24–13 win.

The Whalers finished the 1990s 64-40-1, while NFA went 43-57-1.

11
THE 150TH GAME AND BEYOND

2000–PRESENT

In 2000, the athletic directors at Norwich Free Academy and New London decided that the rivalry needed a permanent date. NFA already played St. Bernard on Thanksgiving, and New London played Fitch, but a special game deserved a special date. Thus, the oldest high school rivalry in the country moved to Thanksgiving Day.

The captains of both schools also held a breakfast the day before the game and would meet in the city that hosted the game every year.

The Wildcats won the first game of the millennium, 19–8, at Cannamela Field. J.J. Justice—whose father, Jim, was a standout for the Wildcats a generation ago—scored a touchdown, as did Gil Ziemba, who also threw a touchdown to Kenny Jones. The Whalers, whose lone score came on an eighty-five-yard pass from Tirike McCoy to Jamar McClellan, scuffled through a 1-8-1 season.

NFA coach Steve Robichaud again had his team on the rise entering 2001. Justice was beginning to show flashes of his athletic talent, something that one day would lead to a four-year career at Maryland. There were also Kenny Jones, Anthony Flanders and Manny Moreno on offense and a young freshman named Matt Shaughnessy on defense.

Norwich was 7-2 entering its final game of the season against New London, which was headed the other way at 2-7. On the final day,

Justice threw two touchdowns, and Flanders rushed for two more in a 34–0 win. Despite the 8-2 mark, NFA just missed the playoffs.

New London rebounded in 2002, going 7-4 in large part due to the arrival of running back Lou Allen. He scored twenty-one touchdowns that season, including two against the Wildcats on November 28. Unfortunately for Allen and the Whalers, NFA scored many more times than that in the game, for a 48–12 win.

NFA back J.J. Justice in 2004. He later became a star defensive back for the University of Maryland. *Courtesy of the* Norwich Bulletin.

In 2002, the Wildcats put together arguably their best season since the 1945 team that last won a state championship. Shaughnessy was a bear at defensive end and as a tight end. Justice ran the offense expertly with his arm and feet. Will Bashelor could run or block with the best of them. Chris Bohara, Manny Moreno, Zach Niland, Terry Dunn—they and many others contributed to an 11-0 regular season.

Defensive end Matt Shaughnessy was one of the best players ever to come out of NFA. He was a four-year starter at the University of Wisconsin and presently plays for the Oakland Raiders. *Courtesy of the* Norwich Bulletin.

In the rivalry game, Justice scored four times, and Shaughnessy had a twenty-eight-yard interception return.

Only West Haven in the Class LL semifinals stopped the Wildcats in a 47–26 game.

Despite the 7-4 mark, Marc Romano replaced Ed Sweeney as coach in 2003. Romano was a New London guy, having played linebacker for the Whalers in the mid-1990s.

The Whalers stumbled to a 2-9 season, losing to NFA 34–6 in the final. In his final high school game, Justice scored three touchdowns, while Chase Chiangi recorded a forty-one-yard fumble return in the win.

In 2004, another standout was about to embark on his final season for NFA. Defensive end Matt Shaughnessy had gotten a lot of attention from college coaches from around the country. The *Norwich Bulletin*'s Steve Nalbandian wrote about the defensive wizard on September 7 of that year:

> *NORWICH—When Matt Shaughnessy was a freshman, one of his teammates was Kenny Jones, a dominant personality and the best player on the team.*
>
> *When Shaughnessy was a sophomore, one of his teammates was Terry Dunn, a dominant defensive end who lined up on the opposite end of the line of scrimmage.*
>
> *When Shaughnessy was a junior, one of his teammates was J.J. Justice, a dominant player and the star of the team.*
>
> *Now Shaughnessy is set to kick off his senior season of football. And there is little doubt that NFA is his team. He is the Wildcats' best player, he's the best player in the ECC and he's quite possibly the best player in the state.*
>
> *There are no more shadows blanketing Matt Shaughnessy. His time has arrived.*
>
> *"We've had some really, really good ones here. Major Williams, J.J. Justice, Bryant Stone, Kenny Jones," Wildcats coach Steve Robichaud said. "If Matt's not the best player that NFA has ever had, he's certainly one of the top two or three, regardless of position. It doesn't really say much, but he's just a football player."*
>
> *"I try not to think too much about it," Shaughnessy said. "It's a little pressure (being the star of the team) but I don't go out there thinking I have to do this or that. I'm taking some stuff J.J. did, especially when it comes to picking a school, and using that."*

Shaughnessy debuted with the NFA varsity midway though his freshman season and started making plays right away.

"We probably should have had him up from the beginning, but a few snaps into his first game and Matt's running guys down from the backside against Ledyard," Robichaud said. "He was starting within two games and he proved himself at that point to be completely capable.

"As a coaching staff, we talked about him, and said that if he ever committed himself to football, he was going to be a Division-I player."

And so he has become one. The 17-year-old stands six feet, six inches tall and has bulked up to 220 pounds. Letters from colleges showing interest in him started coming in during his sophomore season and they haven't stopped. Shaughnessy, a defensive end who is shifting to defensive tackle this season, can currently choose among seven scholarship offers—UConn, Syracuse, Boston College, Indiana, Wisconsin, Michigan State and Purdue—with more sure to roll in as the season progresses. All interested schools have an open mind about what position he'll play, ranging from defensive end to linebacker to tight end. In any case, however, he will need to continue to put on weight.

Shaughnessy said the one school he would love to get an offer from but won't because he doesn't have the grades is Notre Dame. After the Fighting Irish, all schools are created equal in his eyes. Playing close to home won't factor into his decision; neither will playing time right off the bat.

"I wanted to have my decision made by now, but that didn't happen," he said. "I want a school that has my major (criminal justice)."

It's strange for Shaughnessy to think about college. After all, prior to his sophomore year, he had always intended to join the army after high school.

"It was just something that I always wanted to do," he said. "I like the discipline. And it's still something I can do. With the job field that I want to get into, a lot of times you need some experience and that can help me."

He is a mountain of a football player, but he is not a fountain of information. Getting Shaughnessy to talk about himself is akin to getting the nearest wall to talk about itself. He is church-mouse quiet on the surface. His father told Robichaud that as he and Matt made the rounds at a number of Midwest colleges this summer, Matt said about four words on the entire trip.

"Matt is quiet, but not always," Robichaud said. "He has a great sense of humor. It's subtle. He's got that grin where he looks like the Cheshire Cat. He's the guy that is always hiding something of yours, or tapping you on your right shoulder but is standing on your left. He's sneaky."

Maybe so off the field, but Shaughnessy doesn't have the luxury of sneaking up on his opponents, and he truthfully never has. Windham coach Brian Crudden has seen him develop of the last four years.

"We've seen him too much," said Crudden, who will get one more up-close look when the Whippets host the Wildcats Sept. 23. "Wow. He is one tough hombre. He's a man-ster.

"We're going to have to come up with some specialized schemes to slow him down. Shaughnessy is the first guy we'll scout and he's a guy you work your offense around where he is on defense."

Said East Lyme coach Andy Dousis: "When he was a sophomore, we thought we just had to run away from Dunn but we ended up running into trouble running into Shaughnessy. Last year we just ran away from him. That was easier. We double-teamed him, chopped him. He's a strong, fast, tenacious player."

His size, strength and speed (he's run a 4.6-second 40-yard dash) are virtually unmatched in the ECC. In the past, the Wildcats lined him up at defensive end, but teams got around that—sort of—by simply running away from him. They won't have that kind of luxury this year, as Shaughnessy is sliding down the line one spot to defensive tackle (he'll still be at tight end on offense).

"Not much changes for him there," Robichaud said. "We want him rushing the passer. He's going to be a quick, aggressive, physical defensive lineman that we feel we will have a mismatch with. And, you can't run away from him now.

"Matt won't stay blocked. You may have him blocked to start, but it won't stay that way. He's got that great height, but he's not some big slow kid. He has great pop to his system."

According to one Internet service that tracks high school recruits, Shaughnessy is ranked as the 29th-best weak side defensive end in the country and projects as a player who will make an impact on a college team and has pro potential.

Shaughnessy can also be a force on offense. Robichaud gave some thought to moving him into the backfield this season, a position he played as a freshman. But the Wildcats decided to keep things how they were, with sophomore Nick Murphy and junior Marcus Charles getting most of the workload at running back.

But make no mistake, defenses will be aware of where Shaughnessy is when NFA has the ball. In addition to being a tremendous blocker, he has great hands. That was evidenced by a play he made two years ago, on defense of all things.

In NFA's 2002 game against New London on a snowy, icy Thanksgiving Day, Whalers quarterback Shaun Guiney dropped back to pass. He looked right, then threw left when he saw what he thought was an open receiver. Shaughnessy had other plans.

Stuck at the line of scrimmage, maybe 10 feet from Guiney, Shaughnessy leapt into the air, arms fully extended upward, his gloveless hands stretched as high as they could go. He didn't just deflect the pass, then intercept it before falling softly to ground; he flat-out caught it and returned it 28 yards for a touchdown for what was one of the more remarkable plays that could be made at this level.

Duane Maranda was an assistant at East Lyme under Dousis before becoming head coach at St. Bernard last year. He is also part of a coach's program at UConn. Last weekend, when UConn hosted Duke, Shaughnessy visited Maranda at Rentschler Field. Maranda was equally impressed with the way Shaughnessy carried himself as he was with his playing ability.

"We brought him into the locker room and introduced him to a lot of the players, like (Dan) Orlovsky and (Alfred) Fincher," Maranda said. "Matt just had so much respect for the situation. He represented the ECC in a way that made me proud."

It's clear Shaughnessy can handle himself off the field as well as on it. As the season goes on, he will gain the mental edge in knowing that he can physically dominate the opposition.

"I don't go in just thinking I'm going to kick someone's butt," Shaughnessy said. "But I want to get that first hit, let him know how it's going to be all game.

> *"This is a lot of work. I've learned a lot being around the guys that been through this. Terry Dunn taught me so much and I watched how J.J. went through this stuff. But I've still got a lot more stuff to work on."*

The next year, Shaughnessy began a four-year career as a starting defensive lineman for the University of Wisconsin. He currently is a defensive lineman for the Oakland Raiders.

Shaughnessy and the Wildcats, though, ran into a buzz saw on November 25, 2004. On a cold, snowy day at Cannamela Field, the Whalers ended a seven-game losing streak by pulling out a 20–14 win on the strength of quarterback Aaron Bryant. Bryant, who later played at the University of Connecticut, had touchdown runs of seventy-five, three and three yards to snap the skid.

After many years of success, Robichaud stepped down after the season and was replaced by Mark Ambruso. Robichaud soon left to become athletic director at E.O. Smith High School in Storrs, a position that he still holds today.

New London coach Jack Cochran returned to his alma mater to coach the Whalers. He led them to one state title. *Courtesy of the* Norwich Bulletin.

During the 2004–05 offseason, former Whaler Jack Cochran was looking for work. He had coached wildly successful teams at New Britain and Bloomfield, but controversy dogged his programs—player recruiting among the forefront, which is a big no-no in Connecticut.

With Cochran available, New London jumped at the chance. Romano was let go and Cochran brought in, and immediately he found success at New London.

Bringing in David Reed—who later became a receiver for the Baltimore Ravens—and using running back Dan Nurse and freshman quarterback Jordan Reed (David's brother), the Whalers roared out to an 8–1 start when they faced NFA on November 24. The Wildcats didn't stand a chance, losing 34–3 as Jordan Reed threw two touchdowns to David, and Nurse scored three touchdowns and rushed for 240 yards.

The game wasn't without its controversy, however. Wrote the *Day*'s Ned Griffen:

> *Things got heated before the game began because New London officials were upset with the condition of NFA's artificial surface, contending that the hosts didn't do enough to clear the snow away.*
>
> *"I was very disappointed the way this was handled," Whalers coach Jack Cochran said. "This field could have easily been cleared. We had the manpower to do it, and I think it was a disservice to the Norwich Free Academy players and the New London players. This game should've been decided on a dry surface. As you saw, there was a lot of slipping and sliding. If this was grass, it would be one thing.*
>
> *"I just hope that it wasn't something that was done with...what's the right word to say? Malice. I hope it wasn't done with malice."*
>
> *"No comment," NFA coach Mark Ambruso said.*

New London reached the Class S final against the Hyde School of New Haven, but with David Reed being suspended, the Whalers lost 31–13 in their first trip to the state championship in almost twenty years.

The *Bulletin*'s Steve Nalbandian wrote about Cochran's first year:

> *From 1990–2004, the New London High School football team had all of six winning seasons and three of those came between 1990 and 1995.*
>
> *It had been 12 years since the Whalers had been to the CIAC playoffs.*
>
> *So when Jack Cochran was hired in March to be the team's coach, it was done to restore the program's place among the state's elite, where it had been for so long. The question, though, was how soon would it be before the Whalers would be back in the postseason.*
>
> *The answer, surprisingly, is just one.*
>
> *"We put the playoff games on our schedule," Cochran said last week after New London beat Norwich Free Academy 34–3 to improve to 9-1 and clinch a Class S semifinal berth. New London plays at Northwest Catholic at 6:30 on Tuesday night. "That was the goal from the beginning and that will always be the goal.*
>
> *"When I hear coaches talking about wanting to contend or rebuild, I think that's an insult to the kids. Making the playoffs is always the No. 1 goal."*
>
> *Cochran came to New London with a ton of baggage. He had coached Bloomfield and New Britain to a combined seven state titles, but made few friends along the way.*
>
> *His teams put up excessive point totals, he didn't exchange game films with upcoming opponents and he was accused, investigated and then cleared of improperly using funds for the athletic department.*
>
> *Little has changed in those areas now that he's at New London.*
>
> *The Whalers scored 500 points in 10 games this year, including 77 in a Week 1 win over Plainfield and 90 in a Week 8 win over Griswold.*
>
> *More than one coach has complained about not getting game film from Cochran.*
>
> *And he was accused of "recruiting" star receiver David Reed and his brother, quarterback Jordan, from New Britain. The CIAC investigated those charges and cleared him of any wrongdoing.*
>
> *Three different coaches contacted for this story refused to comment on Cochran or his program.*

None of that bothers Cochran, who professes his first loyalties lie with his players. Some of them were thrilled when they heard who their new coach was going to be. Others weren't sure what to think.

"I really didn't know much about Coach Cochran before he got here," said running back Dan Nurse, who rushed for an ECC-high 16 touchdowns and close to 1,000 yards this year. "I was just hoping we could get to the playoffs. Most of the teams I played for before were decent, but didn't finish what we started."

New London just missed out on the playoffs in 2006, going 7-3. A loss on the final day to NFA didn't help, but the weather played a huge role in halting that attack. Heavy rains turned Cannamela Field into a quagmire, and Shareff Champlain's four-yard run in the third quarter was the only score of a 6–0 game.

New London's quarterback Jordan Reed gets past NFA's Mike Winn on Thursday, November 22, 2007, during their game in Norwich. *Courtesy of the* Norwich Bulletin.

New London running back/linebacker Richie Vitale in 2008. *Courtesy of the* Norwich Bulletin.

The Whalers retooled for the 2007 season. Quarterback Jordan Reed led the way, along with running back Dom Griffin, tight end Anthony Schiavone, fullback/linebacker Richie Vitale and linebacker Earl Wilson.

Jemal Davis, who twenty years prior had begun his budding athletic career at NFA, now was its coach, having replaced Ambruso. Still, the Wildcats couldn't hold New London, which rolled over NFA 62–14. Vitale scored five times—four on the ground—and Griffin added three scores. Nearly two weeks later, the 11-0 Whalers went into the Class S championship against old friend Ansonia but didn't stand a chance, losing 35–0.

The Whalers went into 2008 on a hot streak again, going 9-1 into Thanksgiving Day while the Wildcats were 6-3. With Jordan Reed injured, freshman quarterback Casey Cochran—Jack's son—stepped in and threw a touchdown to Schiavone, rushing for a score in a 21–7 win. On December 6, Cochran finally earned a state championship for his alma mater with a 27–18 win over Seymour in the Class SS final.

It also would be Cochran's last game in New London. In early 2009, he was named baseball coach, but it was discovered that he had begun spring practices before the required time set by the Connecticut Interscholastic Athletic Conference, the governing body of high school sports in the state. That move, along with a fight with Fitch coach Jim Buonocore—the son of the former New London great—prior to the 2008 season at a weightlifting event finally forced the New London administration to fire Cochran. In came current coach Jeff Larson, who in his first season led New London to a 34–14 win.

The next year proved to be one of the best games of the twenty-first century. NFA was undefeated (9-0), and New London was 8-1. Both would head to the playoffs, but first came this game in New London.

Backed by touchdowns from Anthony Facchini (fifty-nine yards) and Isaiah Smith (sixty-five yards), along with an Erik Washburn to Colin Smith forty-three-yard pass for a score, the Wildcats won the 149th meeting, 20–14, to complete a 10-0 regular season. Despite the win, NFA fell in the Class LL semifinal two weeks later to Trumbull.

New London, however, won its two playoff games to reach the Class M championship but came up short against Hillhouse, losing 7–0.

On November 24, 2011, the teams met for the 150th game —roughly five hundred yards from where the first game was played 131 years earlier. More than three thousand people lined Norwich's field to watch as the Whalers thrashed the Wildcats, 37–17. Kyle McKinnon scored three touchdowns, and Jevon Elmore added two scores for the Whalers, while Washburn threw two touchdowns for the Wildcats, who, despite the loss, still lead the all-time series, 73-66-11.

12
REMEMBRANCES OF YEARS PAST

Naturally, with so many games, there have been many recollections of past games—the people, the players, the coaches and the atmosphere.

Those affiliated with the game, from both teams, shared their experiences.

Brad Roberts attended Bulkeley High School in the late 1940s:

> *I have some memories from my Bulkeley/NFA days. A few nights during the football season a few friends and I would travel to NFA and go to their Saturday night dances. No problems, just a few enjoyable dances at the Norton Gym during the evening. The games were usually close and attended by a large crowd of local sports fans. There are names that have faded from my memory bank. I didn't see the Bouley brothers play at NFA but got to know Larry in later years. He went on to play at Georgia in the mid-1940s and played with some great Georgia players, Frankie Sinkwich for one and maybe Charlie Trippi. I do remember many good Bulkeley players from years past, but none that stood out particularly in NFA games.*
>
> *I do remember a few interesting things about the competition between the schools. At the old Bulkeley School on the side of the building that housed the Gym next to the cemetery there was a large Red "N" painted*

about two or three stories up where no one could possibly reach it without a good-sized ladder. It stayed there forever because it couldn't be seen unless you walked up the sidewalk between the school and the cemetery. I don't remember any windows on that side of the building. It had a stucco finish, which would have made it nearly impossible to remove the paint. I have no idea what year it would have been painted there.

I do remember about 1949 a group of Bulkeley boys were stopped on their way home by police just outside of Norwich because they had nine or ten boys in their car, and they also had large amounts of orange and black paint (Bulkeley colors) in the trunk of the car. It was discovered that they had painted the wooden doors at NFA orange and black. I don't know what happened to them. But I learned today from another Bulkeley boy I talked with this evening, that he had been asked to join the group going to do the paint job but refused. He said that days later the students at Bulkeley were asked to contribute money toward the cleanup job at NFA. He said he refused. So I guess the school was asked to clean up the mess.

I do miss those days, and I have always felt that I was really lucky to have been a "Bulkeley boy." I'm still attending the yearly "All Classes" reunions at Ocean Beach. I've enjoyed running my last three class reunions, the fiftieth, fifty-fifth and the sixtieth in 2010.

Bob McPhail played for Bulkeley in the late 1940s and later went to work at Norwich Free Academy as the school's athletic director and assistant football coach. As of this writing, McPhail still is connected to the school and is the golf coach:

There was a point in time when three of the football coaches at Norwich Free Academy all graduated the same year from Bulkeley School. Jim Giordano, who was the head coach, and myself—I worked with the defensive backs—and Dan Driscoll, who was the freshman coach.

[Coming back to coach against New London], *you don't lose that completely, or it takes a longer period of time. You like to see both teams play well. Certainly while I was coaching, I was more interested in winning than seeing anybody representing New London play better than us.*

Bob Demars played on the line for NFA in the late 1950s and early 1960s, playing a role on the 1961 league championship team. Just prior to the game against New London in 1961, he remembered an extraordinary bit of impromptu school spirit that took hold:

> *It was Friday of the New London week. We hadn't beaten New London in a few years, so that made it even bigger. Every day we did a different event that was planned...something on Tuesday; Thursday we had a special edition of the* [school newspaper] Red and White. *Friday, they had a pep rally or a bonfire scheduled for that night.*
>
> *Back when we were there, during the lunch period* [on Friday], *the band used to practice over on Chelsea Parade. For some reason, they came in and when they marched on campus, kids were out on lunch and fell in behind them. Bennett Edwards, who was a great guy, the band director, he just took off and went in front of the Main building and over on the sidewalk over by MT* [Manual Training building], *and as he was going, he was picking up more kids.*
>
> *He went to the back parking lot, along by the bleachers and got more kids, and he got to the Commercial* [building], *and at that point in time word must have spread because kids were just coming out of class. Teachers were letting their class go, and the teachers that didn't, the kids said, "The hell with it, we're going anyway." Then it worked its way back to the archway* [between Slater Museum and the Converse Art Gallery] *and went back around between Main and Slater, and it was like the whole freaking school was there, and I think there was 2,600, 2,700 kids at the time.*
>
> *It was all impromptu. Nothing was planned, and it was unbelievable. George Shattuck* [the principal] *was out there as a part of it. It ended up, I believe, on the lawn in front of the Main building with a couple of songs, and then someone said it was time to go back to class, and people just went right back to class with no problems. It was the most unbelievable thing.*
>
> *Of course, the afternoon was shot for the teachers, but I mean you had just about every kid in the school following the band.*

Leo Bawza played for NFA in the late 1960s and recalled that there was no bigger rival than the one to the south of Norwich:

> *Ohio State and Michigan? Army and Navy? Yankees and Red Sox? Rivalries to be sure. Like NFA and New London? No. Think more like the Hatfields and the McCoys…the Earps and the Clantons, where violence will break out whenever the parties meet. No one remembers why they should hate or knows who did what to whom, or what was the original cause of the animosity. Doesn't matter… it just is what it is. And so with NFA and New London…it is what it is. It was like that before the USS* Maine *was sunk in Havana Harbor, before Teddy Roosevelt charged up San Juan Hill. Christ… before light bulbs and automobiles.*
>
> *I started at NFA like everyone else…thirteen years old, scared witless of its college campus size and pre-traumatized by rumors of freshman hazing. What if I don't fit in? What if I don't make any friends? No worry, as it turned out. By Christmas I had something in common with each of the other 3,200 students. We all hated the green and yellow of New London. NFA's 12-week hate New London immersion course, like an intense dog obedience school, was successful for the 100th consecutive year. Of course, it would take three and a half years of rallies and banners and follow-up instruction from the school to make it truly ingrained.*
>
> *It was a different time. Shorts were short, you didn't thump your chest after doing your job on the field and you just dropped the football after scoring. We belonged to the now-defunct CDC, the Capitol District Conference. In the late 1960s, this conference included New Britain, Enfield, East Hartford, Hartford Public, Hartford Weaver, Hartford Buckley, Waterford and New London. I played baseball and football against some of the toughest teams in the state. They were big schools, and we were proud to beat them. I learned during freshman year to play hard. I learned when we played New London to play harder. In baseball, you slid into home on a close play. Against New London, you went in standing and took the catcher out. In football, you juked and spun away from a tackler. Against New London, you lowered your head and aimed*

for their breastbone. Because they wore green and yellow, it was not enough to win individual battles; you had to physically beat them up in the process to prove you were tougher. You didn't trash talk in football. You hit someone, anyone, hard enough to knock them out of the game. Over and over, play after play. No talk. We were told New London had "bounties" on certain players. Knock us out of the game, and they collect their bounty. The bounty rumor pissed us off and did more to motivate us than it did them. Hell, for all I know, our own coaches started the rumor and used it as part of our "psychological preparation." Physically, we were ready for the late-in-the-year match-up, so the coaches simply put in a few new plays and spent the rest of the week stoking our fires.

Night before the game? No sleep. Get to the clubhouse early on game day to get taped. Watch your buddies throw up like they're in a landing craft heading to the beach at Normandy. Then the game. So much adrenalin you ignore the ankle sprain you just got. You pop your buddy's dislocated finger back into place in the huddle because he won't leave the game. Carry the ball, get the stuffing knocked out of you, gain four or five yards, puke in your mask and then do it thirty-four more times. When a substitute comes in for you…you throw his ass off the field because you are not leaving. This is New London. One shot a year at this. You know you are going to be pissing blood for two days, and it doesn't matter. This is your whole season, and there is no reason to leave anything on the field.

Bob Roche played for NFA in the 1966 game, which was the 100th game of the rivalry:

An amusing anecdote that I recall from then is that the captain of our cheerleading squad, Mary Ellen Kelley, was dating a New London player, George Gerhardt.

After we lost by a couple of touchdowns, the next day the Bulletin *published an article covering the game and included a picture of Mary Ellen and George walking off the field together arm and arm.*

Needless to say, as seventeen-year-olds, if we didn't feel emasculated enough after the final score, we certainly did after your readers saw that picture.

Jim Buonocore was a pint-sized halfback for Chapman Tech who played in the New London High School–NFA game in 1951, the first year after the merger of Chapman and Bulkeley. Buonocore spent time as a successful assistant coach at NFA before returning to New London in 1969, coaching the team for the next thirty years and collecting four state championships and 208 wins. He recalled the first time he went against NFA in 1969:

> *The* [New London principal, Bill Foye] *came over the house; he lived like five houses away on Montauk Avenue. I'm out in front of the house, and he toots the horn to come over to the car. He says, "Jim, how'd you like to be the football coach next year at New London?" I said, "Mr. Foye, what are you talking about?" He says, "Well, we've got an opening and I have to recommend a coach next Thursday to the Board of Ed."*
>
> *So I said I gotta see what my wife* [Candace] *says. He said, "All right, I'll wait in the car."*
>
> *He must have heard her because she said, "You're not going! They never cared about you!" I said this is an opportunity to come back, and she said, 'You're crazy! I wouldn't go if I were you. Tell him you don't want the job and you're staying in Norwich."*
>
> *I come out and said, "OK, Mr. Foye, I'll take it." And Thursday, they named me the coach.*
>
> *Playing Norwich that first year…if someone slaps you, you feel it. Every time they got hit, I felt it. It was very, very hard. I knew where I lived and that was it. Biggest game of the year for Norwich, and us, too.*
>
> *NFA went ahead with a field goal with two minutes to go, and it wasn't looking good for us. I called timeout, and I called* [Tim] *Lewis over. I had a junior team, all juniors. They were tough kids. I said, "This is what we've got to do." I had good receivers, so I wanted to pass the first play, and they went after Lewis. Boy, he didn't have any time to breathe; they killed him.*
>
> *We're back again on the forty-yard line, and I called time out. OK, I want to run this play where everyone goes this way, and the quarterback goes behind him because he can run. Nobody—if you ever show it to*

> *me, I'll believe it—pulls the center. Well, we pulled the center. Richie Foye. So here's Richie, and the team goes this way, Richie pulls out here, Lewis spins around and comes here and there he is behind Richie, and down the sidelines they went—touchdown. That's how we beat Norwich that day.*

Tommie Major was a top-rate linebacker for New London who went on to play at Maryland State College, now known as Maryland-Eastern Shore. The Major name is synonymous with football excellence at New London, and Tommie was one of the most feared defensive players ever to come out of that school. He remains involved with the Whalers as an assistant coach today:

> *The difference between nowadays and back in the day is that you almost have to inform kids that you have to compete. Back when I was playing, I don't think the coaches really had to do that. We wanted to play. That's the main thing. Kids nowadays are big and strong and fast, but you really go back to the mental aspect of it. The main thing is teaching them how to compete.*
>
> *In many ways,* [playing under coaches Bob Weiss and Jim Buonocore] *was two different teams, two different philosophies. You had one person who was brought up as a New London person and knew the environment and knew the experiences. You had another guy who came in, young, brashy-type guy, who was a great motivator. Two different styles and two different coaches.*
>
> *This year, I had the opportunity to be a guest speaker at NFA. I tell you, it was one of the greatest moments of my life; it really was. It's just an institution that you can really be proud of. That's what makes that rivalry so great. The campus is great. New London High has a tradition that can't be duplicated by any other, and Norwich has that campus mystique.*

Jim Giordano was a New London guy who came to be one of the best coaches in NFA history. He played at Bulkeley and came back to coach the Wildcats for ten years in the 1960s and 1970s:

> *Well, when you think about the oldest high school rivalry in the country, it's pretty astounding.*
>
> *The games themselves, they were well attended. I ended up coaching at NFA, and the 1968 game was very exciting. New London was undefeated at the time. For attendance, eight thousand people were a lot of people in those days. There was a lot of interest in the game. It was a very unique rivalry, I would say.*
>
> *To add more irony to it, I left NFA in '81, and I became principal at New London High School. It was like coming back home.*

Kent Reyes played quarterback and kicker for New London in the early 1970s. A hulking figure, Reyes has been a firefighter for the city of New London for the past twenty-plus years and is an assistant coach with the football team:

> [The rivalry] *goes beyond my time, because I followed New London High School football as a kid. I saw Dave Connors play against NFA. I saw John Brennan play against NFA. My interest was piqued early because of all the guys that grew up in my neighborhood who were quarterbacks, like Billy Discordia, John Brennan and Tim Lewis. It was easy for me to want to be a quarterback.*
>
> [The guys on NFA] *were also decent friends of mine. They weren't guys that we hated. I got recruited to a lot of different schools with Jimmy Justice, and we became very good friends. Ronnie Delgado and I were very good friends, and Bobby Perry and I were very good friends. Jimmy Leone and I had a big mutual respect. Even though people make a scene worse than what it is when it becomes a rivalry, when you become interpersonal, and you see guys one-on-one, all that stuff goes away because the acquaintance and the friendships start to develop once you see each other as humans and not adversaries.*
>
> *It may be only thirteen miles apart, but it seemed like it was just next door to us because* [we were able to] *go to NFA and hang out with Jimmy Justice and hang out with Ronnie and be friends with them at the same time. I competed against these guys since seventh-, eighth-grade basketball, different leagues like that, and still being able to maintain friendships as we got older, which is much more important than football.*

Jemal Davis played at NFA in the late 1980s and then twenty years later came back to coach his alma mater. He was born and raised in New London until he was ten years old, when he moved to Norwich:

> *It was a game of family rivalries, of friends that I knew that I grew up with since I was ten...When I looked across the field, a lot of those guys I grew up with. So it was that kind of relationship.*
>
> *In terms of the magnitude and the storied history of it, I don't think I really came to appreciate that until I was actually in college and then later on as a coach.*
>
> *My college roommate was Jason Appleby, who played at New London. In college, I came to appreciate it just because we would talk about our games against one other to other members of the team, and we would kind of reflect in terms of, hey, we played in the oldest high school rivalry. Guys from Florida and Pennsylvania, those states that typically are known for football, we had that as something to say, in Connecticut, a place you guys might not typically think to have one of the earliest places to commit to having a rivalry, actually did—so that was something that was very special.*

Ambrose Fletcher was a stellar running back at New London in the early 1990s, leading the Whalers to two state championships. He attended Penn State and was a running back for Joe Paterno, helping the Nittany Lions win the 1995 Rose Bowl over Oregon:

> *For me, back then, it was kind of hard to picture it as a real rivalry because we used to beat up on Norwich* [New London won fourteen in a row between 1983 and 1996]. *I noticed the last couple of years that Norwich had some really good programs coming through there.*
>
> *For us, from practice and game-wise, it was always their best players against our best players.*
>
> *Regardless of what game we played, it was always "Watch out for the Fletcher brothers."* [Kasi, Ambrose's brother, was a year older.] *"One of them is out of the game, we know who's getting the ball."*
>
> *I've been back to Connecticut a few times, and I know it's a big game and a big rivalry game. I remember when I first graduated, how*

much everyone talked about that being the rivalry game, Norwich and New London. Even when we were in high school, it was a big deal that Norwich and New London was the oldest game. It was something that we did know about, but...to me, I don't know about anyone else, we always tried to play our best every game.

Steve Robichaud coached NFA from 1993 to 2004, leading the Wildcats into the state playoffs in 1998 for the first time in school history. In 1997, NFA beat New London to snap a fourteen-game losing streak on a wild second-half comeback:

> *I can remember, I felt we had a pretty good team that year. We didn't play* [New London] *on Thanksgiving; we played St. Bernard on Thanksgiving at that time. I think we opened up with New London down there, and again, it was kind of one of those things where there was an aura about New London that was kind of hard describe. I wasn't an NFA person; I didn't know a whole lot about NFA–New London other than they were kind of neighboring towns and there was a rivalry that had been going on over the years. Again, I wasn't close to that way of thinking, but there certainly was an aura about New London.*
>
> *We went down there, and all of a sudden we're down 19–0 at the half. We're talking to the kids at halftime, and we're saying, "Hey, we're a pretty good football team here. There's no reason we should be down 19–0," and I don't think they* [New London] *had a great team, but it was almost as if our kids went in there and weren't really confident about what they could do.*
>
> *All I can remember is in the second half, we did go out there, played well, shut them out and we won the game 20–19. The thing that kind of still sticks with me is I remember Bryant Stone scoring our last touchdown and him going into the end zone, and he raised the ball up and got flagged by the official. So now we're going in, and it's 19–19, and Major Williams has to kick a thirty-five-yard PAT for us to ahead. And as Major always did, he kicked it, and we won the game 20–19, and you might have thought we won the Super Bowl.*

We were certainly ecstatic about the win, but it was a win, we were 1-0. OK, it was New London, I understand that, but it didn't really register it was any bigger deal. That following Monday, the superintendent [Mary Lou Bargnesi] *comes into the gym where I was teaching—at that time, it was still early in the school year, so all the kids in PE class were kind of getting things going, getting them organized—they were just sitting in the bleachers. She comes in and addresses the whole group about the New London win. And that kind of set in. "Oh, I guess this is bigger than I thought."*

ABOUT THE AUTHOR

Brian Girasoli was the assistant sports editor at the *Norwich Bulletin* from 2002 to 2007 and currently holds that post again, since 2010. He is a graduate of the University of Connecticut (BA, English), Quinnipiac University (MS, Journalism) and, come the end of 2012, Sacred Heart University (teacher certification, secondary English). He is also a past president of the Connecticut Sports Writers' Alliance. The Norwich Free Academy v. New London rivalry holds a special place for him as a graduate of Norwich Free Academy (class of 1994).